W9-BMY-173

Writing the Critical Essay

ANIMAL RIGHTS

An OPPOSING VIEWPOINTS® Guide

Terry O'Neill, *Book Editor*

Bruce Glassman, *Vice President*
Bonnie Szumski, *Publisher, Series Editor*
Helen Cothran, *Managing Editor*

OPPOSING
VIEWPOINTS®
SERIES

GREENHAVEN PRESS
An imprint of Thomson Gale, a part of The Thomson Corporation

THOMSON
GALE

Detroit • New York • San Francisco • San Diego • New Haven, Conn. • Waterville, Maine • London • Munich

© 2006 Thomson Gale, a part of The Thomson Corporation.

Thomson and Star Logo are trademarks and Gale and Greenhaven Press are registered trademarks used herein under license.

For more information, contact
Greenhaven Press
27500 Drake Rd.
Farmington Hills, MI 48331-3535
Or you can visit our Internet site at http://www.gale.com

ALL RIGHTS RESERVED.
No part of this work covered by the copyright hereon may be reproduced or used in any form or by any means—graphic, electronic, or mechanical, including photocopying, recording, taping, Web distribution or information storage retrieval systems—without the written permission of the publisher.

Every effort has been made to trace the owners of copyrighted material.

LIBRARY OF CONGRESS CATALOGING-IN-PUBLICATION DATA

Animal rights / Terry O'Neill, book editor.
   p. cm. — (Writing the critical essay)
  Includes bibliographical references and index.
  ISBN 0-7377-3194-X (lib. : alk. paper)
  1. Animal rights. I. O'Neill, Terry, 1944– . II. Series
  HV4708.A543 2006
  179'.3—dc22
                                 2005042395

Printed in the United States of America

CONTENTS

Section Three: Supporting Research Material

Examining the state of writing and how it is taught in the United States was the official purpose of the National Commission on Writing in America's Schools and Colleges. The commission, made up of teachers, school administrators, business leaders, and college and university presidents, released its first report in 2003. "Despite the best efforts of many educators," commissioners argued, "writing has not received the full attention it deserves." Among the findings of the commission was that most fourth-grade students spent less than three hours a week writing, that three-quarters of high school seniors never receive a writing assignment in their history or social studies classes, and that more than 50 percent of first-year students in college have problems writing error-free papers. The commission called for a "cultural sea change" that would increase the emphasis on writing for both elementary and secondary schools. These conclusions have made some educators realize that writing must be emphasized in the curriculum. As colleges are demanding an ever-higher level of writing proficiency from incoming students, schools must respond by making students more competent writers. In response to these concerns, the SAT, an influential standardized test used for college admissions, required an essay for the first time in 2005.

Books in the Writing the Critical Essay: An Opposing Viewpoints Guide series use the patented Opposing Viewpoints format to help students learn to organize ideas and arguments and to write essays using common critical writing techniques. Each book in the series focuses on a particular type of essay writing—including expository, persuasive, descriptive, and narrative—that students learn while being taught both the five-paragraph essay as well as longer pieces of writing that have an opinionated focus. These guides include everything necessary to help students research, outline, draft, edit, and ultimately write successful essays across the curriculum, including essays for the SAT.

Using Opposing Viewpoints

This series is inspired by and builds upon Greenhaven Press's acclaimed Opposing Viewpoints series. As in the parent series, each book in the Writing the Critical Essay series focuses on a timely and controversial social issue that provides lots of opportunities for creating thought-provoking essays. The first section of each volume begins with a brief introductory essay that provides context for the opposing viewpoints that follow. These articles are chosen for their accessibility and clearly stated views. The thesis of each article is made explicit in the article's title and is accentuated by its pairing with an opposing or alternative view. These essays are both models of persuasive writing techniques and valuable research material that students can mine to write their own informed essays. Guided reading and discussion questions help lead students to key ideas and writing techniques presented in the selections.

The second section of each book begins with a preface discussing the format of the essays and examining characteristics of the featured essay type. Model five-paragraph and longer essays then demonstrate that essay type. The essays are annotated so that key writing elements and techniques are pointed out to the student. Sequential, step-by-step exercises help students construct and refine thesis statements; organize material into outlines; analyze and try out writing techniques; write transitions, introductions, and conclusions; and incorporate quotations and other researched material. Ultimately, students construct their own compositions using the designated essay type.

The third section of each volume provides additional research material and writing prompts to help the student. Additional facts about the topic of the book serve as a convenient source of supporting material for essays. Other features help students go beyond the book for their research. Like other Greenhaven Press books, each book in the Writing the Critical Essay series includes bibliographic listings of relevant periodical articles, books, Web sites, and organizations to contact.

Writing the Critical Essay: An Opposing Viewpoints Guide will help students master essay techniques that can be used in any discipline.

Background to Controversy: Animal Rights

From the beginning of human history, people have tamed and lived with animals. Animals are companions as well as sources of protection, food, clothing, transportation, sport (such as hunting and racing), entertainment (such as in circuses), and labor (such as to pull plows and wagons and to carry loads). For centuries, the relationship between humans and their domesticated animals was rarely questioned: People used animals in the ways they needed to. But by the nineteenth century, some people began to question this relationship. They saw people abusing their work animals by beating them, feeding them poorly, and providing them with no shelter or poor shelter. If an animal became sick or too old to work, many people simply left it to die. Animals were also used in cruel sports such as bullbaiting, in which a dog fought a tethered bull. In response, in 1824 a small group of people in England formed the Society for the Prevention of Cruelty to Animals. This group managed to get a few laws passed forbidding cruel treatment of animals.

The ASPCA

In the United States Henry Bergh, a wealthy philanthropist who was also outraged by cruelty to animals, believed these conditions should be changed. Bergh was responsible for forming the American Society for the Prevention of Cruelty to Animals (ASPCA) in New York in 1866. Similar organizations were formed in Philadelphia and Boston shortly after, and by 1888 most states had their own humane organizations and animal shelters. Thirty-seven of the thirty-eight states had passed laws prohibiting some kind of cruelty to animals.

Since ancient times, people have trained animals like this white tiger to perform in carnivals and circuses.

Initially formed to aid work animals, such as the horses who pulled carriages and hauled goods, the ASPCA's goal was to end the beatings, inadequate food, and poor housing that many of these animals suffered.

They also worked to establish humane standards for treatment of animals used for vivisection—that is, medical experimentation in which an animal is operated on in some way. In 1892 the American Humane Organization was responsible for getting laws passed to prevent the use of animals in repetitive experiments for "teaching or demonstrating well-known accepted facts."[1]

Animals as Property

Not everyone agreed that animals needed the protection of organizations such as the ASPCA. Many people believed

1. Max Weber, "The Animal Rights Movement," http://maxweber.hunter.cuny.edu.

that animals were people's property and that individuals should be able to treat their property any way they wanted. They did not want the government or other organizations interfering with their personal property rights. They reinforced their position by pointing to Bible passages such as this one from Genesis: "Let [humans] have dominion over the fish of the sea, and over the fowl of the air, and over the cattle, and over all the earth, and over every creeping thing that creepeth upon the earth."

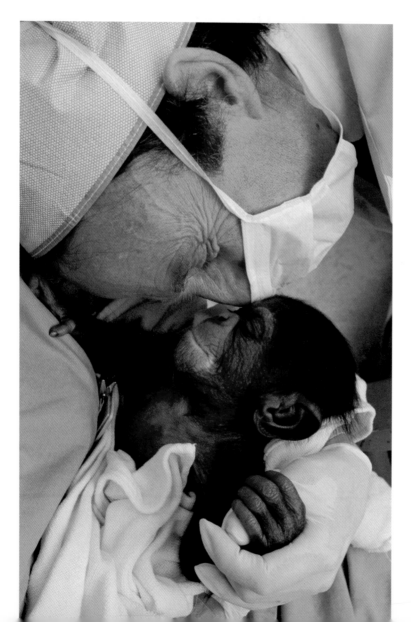

A veterinarian interacts with a chimpanzee being used for AIDS research.

The Animal Rights Movement

In 1973 a philosophy professor named Peter Singer published an essay called "Animal Liberation" in the *New York Review of Books* that led to the birth of the modern animal rights movement. The article became the basis for Singer's book with the same title, published in 1975. Singer's ideas went far beyond treating animals humanely. He asserted that animals have rights beyond basic welfare. In fact Singer and many animal rights proponents believe that it is unethical for humans to own or make use of animals in any way because human ownership, no matter how well intended, interferes with an animal's right to live according to its nature. As one animal rights advocate says:

> The animal rights movement seeks nothing less than the complete transformation of our relationship with other species, from one based on ownership and exploitation to one based on a guardianship model, in which all human relationships must be based on what is in the best interest of animals, not humans. . . . The animal rights movement seeks to create legal protections for animals . . . as stepping stones on the way to the total liberation of animals.[2]

Animal Rights Today

Today, those who advocate for animals can be divided roughly into two groups: those who stand for animal welfare and those who stand for animal rights.

Welfarists accept that animals will be used by humans for various purposes, but they insist that animals be treated as humanely as possible. So, for example, if animals must be used for food, they should be raised in a humane

2. Pete [no last name given], "Animal Rights vs. Animal Welfare," San Francisco Indymedia, January 19, 2005, http://sf.indymedia.org.

manner and killed without cruelty. If they must be used in research, they should be allowed pain-free, humane existences.

Rightists do not accept that humans need to use animals. They encourage people to practice vegetarianism, wear no animal skins (fur and leather), find substitutes for animals in research, and eliminate animal entertainment such as circuses, zoos, and horse racing. One segment of the animal rights movement believes that even breaking the law (such as releasing lab animals from labs,

Dressed in monkey outfits, animal rights supporters protest the use of monkeys in sound-blasting experiments.

Signs on dogs read: "RACE CARS NOT ME!" and "I RUN ON THE BEACH NOW!"

In 1999 animal rights activists sit with greyhound dogs on the steps of the statehouse in Boston to support a bill to ban greyhound racing in Massachusetts.

minks from mink farms, and vandalizing research institutions) is acceptable to gain rights for animals, just as some would argue that lawbreaking is acceptable in the pursuit of rights for humans.

The Animal Welfare Act

Thanks to the animal rights movement, many laws have been passed to protect animals. A major milestone was the 1966 Animal Welfare Act, which regulated the way animals such as cats, dogs, and chimpanzees were used in research labs. It provided for veterinary care, facility inspections, and specific standards of treatment. It did not, however, cover small animals such as rats, mice, and birds. Later versions of the law covered not only laboratory conditions but also treatment of animals in exhibitions (such as at zoos and circuses), during transport, and by dealers. In 2000 Congress proposed adding rats, mice, and birds to the act's protection. This was implemented in 2002.

Other laws prohibit dog- and cockfighting and other violent animal sports, regulate the horse- and dog-racing industries, and prohibit animal abuse and neglect by individual pet owners. Many animal rights advocates say that these laws do not go far enough. They say that many animals are suffering and living in unnatural conditions and should be protected or liberated from humans entirely.

The Issues

Animal rights issues involve a wide spectrum of topics, including the use of animals for food, clothing, and entertainment; animals used in medical and other research; the keeping of pets; farm animal welfare; hunting and fishing; zoos; breeding; product testing; cloning; and ecology and loss of natural habitat. It also covers philosophical discussions such as whether rats or fruit flies deserve the same rights as chimpanzees, and whether any of these deserve the same rights as humans. In this book, you will find essays debating several of these issues and will receive guidance in writing your own essay about animal rights.

Section One:
Opposing
Viewpoints on
Animal Rights

Animals Have Rights

Julie Cohen

As part of an article she was researching, writer Julie Cohen visited the Georgia State University Language Research Center and met Panbanisha, a fourteen-year-old ape who communicates through an electronic keyboard. In the following article, Cohen describes how Panbanisha's apparent ability to think and to carry on a conversation made Cohen reconsider her beliefs about animal rights. Panbanisha shows her that apes may be closer to humans than she had previously thought. Additional research showed her that other animals, too, have the ability to think and express feelings. These two qualities are often cited as particularly human qualities and, Cohen suggests, may lead to more legal rights for at least some species of animals.

Consider the following questions:
1. Why is Cohen impressed that the Harvard and Georgetown law schools have started offering courses in animal rights law?
2. Why is the author impressed when Panbanisha expresses sadness?

Sitting on the forest floor opposite a haughty female ape I was completely taken aback when she tipped her head on one side and as she pressed the buttons on an electronic keyboard, a synthesised voice said, "Has the visitor brought a surprise?" Thankfully Bill, a researcher at the Georgia State University Language Research Centre came to my aid saying, "Yes, yes she has—she brought you some jello." "Good," came the satisfied response.

Julie Cohen, "Monkey Puzzles," *Geographical*, vol. 72, May 2000, p. 58. Copyright © 2000 by Campion Interactive Publishing Ltd. Reproduced by permission.

Sue Savage-Rumbaugh, a research scientist at Georgia State University, plays with Nyota, a pygmy chimpanzee.

Before visiting Sue Savage-Rumbaugh and her talented team of researchers at the Georgia State University Language Research Centre I would have been cautious to suggest animals deserved legal rights. I would have agreed that anti-cruelty rules are too weak and that animals need to be treated with kindness, respect and care, but legal rights for animals may have seemed too extreme. But spending an afternoon in the company of Panbanisha, a 14-year-old bonobo, or pygmy chimpanzee, and her one-year-old baby, Nyota, convinced me otherwise.

Legal Rights for Animals?

For years animal rights groups have put forward the case for legal rights but it is only now that demands are being taken seriously. Last term, Harvard and Georgetown Law Schools began teaching a new course in animal rights law. That the two most prestigious law schools in the USA are taking this new field of law seriously gives an indication of the change in public feeling. Animals have always been regarded as property under both American and British law. But as Steven Wise, the charismatic lawyer teaching the new Harvard Law School course on animal rights law explains, we should challenge our conceptions.

"What is it that makes humans qualify for legal rights and not animals?" he asks. "In Greek and Roman times humans were deemed superior because they believed God had designed a hierarchical world where humans were dominant. Animals were for human use. They were regarded as mere property. That has stuck in the eyes of the law and yet it is a principle without intellectual foundation. Darwin showed that the world was created in a far more random way and that humans are not superior to anything by divine decree."

Wise points out previous misconceptions that have now been remedied. Women were considered inferior to men until relatively recently and for many years black people were not allowed equal rights to white people. This illustrates how wrong our conceptions have been in the past. If the way women and black people were treated had not been challenged then the inequalities would have continued.

Talking Animals

Panbanisha is lucky. It is clear from her attitude she is in no doubt that she is a star and uses this celebrity status to her benefit as much as possible.

When the photographer asked to take her picture a delicate negotiation process had to be undertaken. "You're beautiful," he told her in very embarrassed whispers. She

was pleased. "I'll bring you a drink," he offered seeing that he was getting her interest. "Coffee, milk and juice with ice," she demanded, clearly delighted.

From that moment on she had the photographer and I obeying her every whim. Before she would answer questions about what she likes to eat and do she insisted on playing hide-and-seek in the woods belonging to the centre.

Ares. © by Cagle Cartoons, Inc. Reproduced by permission.

Panbanisha communicates by pointing to symbols on a chart. Scientists at Georgia State University claim that some primates can interact with humans on a number of levels.

The simple questions I asked her were clearly way below her capacity as she demonstrated when she astounded me by expressing her sadness that Kanzi, a male bonobo she lives alongside, was upset at being left out.

Who would have considered that an animal was capable of expressing feeling for another animal? Panbanisha demonstrated that we should not judge an animal's consciousness by their language ability. That they may not be able to talk does not necessarily mean they cannot understand or think. . . .

Different Rights for Different Species?

But just how far are we going to take this concept of giving animals legal rights? The animal rights law advocates are not claiming that every species deserves the same legal rights. The case must be examined for different species. . . .

In October [1999] New Zealand's Parliament achieved a world-first when it passed legislation prohibiting the use of all great apes in research, testing or teaching unless such use is "in the best interests of the non-human hominid" or "in the interests of the species to which it belongs." That primates should have a right to life, liberty and freedom from torture on the basis of scientific evidence that they not only share our genes but also demonstrate self-awareness and cognitive, emotional and social capacities, is an argument rapidly gaining ground.

Maybe if you'd had a conversation with an ape, you'd agree.

Analyze the essay:
1. After reading about the author's experience, what qualities do you think should make a species eligible for legal rights?
2. Do you agree that animals should have the same rights as people? What limitations, if any, would you put on this? Explain.

Animals Do Not Have Rights

J. Neil Schulman

J. Neil Schulman is a writer and the founder of a publishing company that distributes paperless books through personal computers. He believes that the efforts of some animal rights activists to establish legal rights for animals are foolish. In the following article he discusses his reasons. He says that humans are dominant on this planet and that animals cannot and do not ask for rights; therefore, we should not give them any. He says that animals are not legally competent and could not participate in a court hearing over their rights. Schulman also says that animal rights advocates are more interested in bringing down humankind than in raising up animals. He concludes by listing fifty things that are normal parts of human life but that animals cannot do, thereby proving their inferiority.

Consider the following questions:
1. List the three reasons the author gives for not giving animals rights.
2. According to the author, what does a controversy need?

L et me begin by pointing out a few self-evident facts— in other words, facts that can't be denied (other than as meaningless noise) by anyone advocating for elevating the status of animals.

First, human beings are the dominant species on this planet, making decisions regarding use of the land, the sea,

J. Neil Schulman, "Fifty Things Animals Can't Do," www.maninnature.com, December 7, 2000. Copyright © 2000 by J. Neil Schulman. Reproduced by permission.

A clown from the Barnum and Bailey circus rides an elephant through the streets of New York to the delight of onlookers.

the air, and the near space above the air. Man rules and animals have to take what we do with them and lump it.

Second, there are no animals petitioning mankind, their "oppressor," for an elevated status or recognition of their rights.

Third, this entire discussion is made by some human beings attempting to play on the ethics and esthetics of other human beings so as to cause them to alter the way they act with respect to animals. . . .

Animals Cannot Testify on Their Own Behalf

An animal-rights advocate is in the position of a lawyer bringing a case to court, with a species of animal or representative of that species as the client. A petition for animal rights is, in effect, a petition for emancipation for species, and members of species, that are currently the legal wards of mankind at best—and our outright property without proof there is even standing to consider them as candidates for a conservatorship. It is a case which is brought by the lawyer without either request or even understanding by the client. Moreover, even if we could somehow raise the intelligence and communication abilities of an animal to make it cognizant of the possibility, we don't even know whether their natural metaphysics would prefer dominion over themselves or continued rule by mankind, their "gods."

But let's say we're going to make a court case out of this anyway, without the animal's consent or understanding.

First up would be the question of the court's jurisdiction—and it is undisputed that mankind rules this planet. There is nothing to even question our jurisdiction except another one of our own species—and that fact reinforces, rather than undercuts, the unquestioned jurisdiction of mankind in deciding any question of animal rights.

Animals Do Not and Cannot Contest Their Status

Next up is the question of standing—being able to go into court and make a claim for emancipation on one's own behalf in the first place—and that goes to the question of competence. We would need a competency hearing to begin a trial of emancipation. A human judge is going to come up with the decisive criteria because there's no other life form we can ask to present a friend-of-the-court brief. The competency hearing prior to an emancipation hearing has to pass human-derived criteria because there aren't any other criteria being offered.

And that's where we have an impossible problem. Find me another species whom we can ask and we can have a controversy about the standards we will use in a proposed trial of animal rights—or even conservatorship beyond being mere property. A controversy requires two or more parties. There is only one species capable of taking up the question.

The very thing the animal-rights advocate wants to challenge—that human beings have a monopoly on rights and adjudication of rights—has no being affected by the outcome even laying claim to a contest.

That ends the question of standing for a species, or a member of a species, of animal before it starts.

Given that there are no animals contesting their status as inferiors to mankind, where can a human advocate of animal emancipation possibly go from there? I see only one answer to that question: an attack on the rights of man for no reason other than to oppose the rights of man. It is not for the sake of animal elevation that animal rights is proposed. It is the degradation, population reduction, disempowerment, starvation, and state domination of human beings that is the only possible agenda of animal-rights advocates. They don't love animals. They hate men. . . .

Asay. © 1996 by Creators Syndicate, Inc. Reproduced by permission.

Fifty Things Animals Cannot Do

So, for the sake of not having to debate this anymore, with countless people who don't have any practice in the use and understanding of logical argument, let me now, off the top of my head, present fifty observable activities in which human beings engage that human beings have not observed in any other species. And before you argue with me that you dressed up your cat in human clothes for a fashion show, I mean in all cases: in a state of nature, without human intervention.

English huntsmen and their hounds prepare for a fox hunt, a favorite sport among the British upper class.

1. Writing and reading. 2. Mathematical calculation. 3. Making and playing of musical instruments. 4. Creating and using a calendar. 5. Engaging in commerce. 6. The practice of law. 7. The practice of medicine and veterinary medicine. 8. Pyrotechnics. 9. Cooking food. 10. Studying. 11. Tracking the movements of celestial bodies. 12. Whale watching. 13. The use of graphic arts. 14. Provision of artificial light. 15. Provision of artificial heat. 16. Home decoration. 17. Modeling clothing. 18. Making jewelry. 19. Fashion design. 20. Plumbing. 21. Telegraphy. 22. Telephony. 23. Broadcasting. 24. Furniture design. 25. The practice of religion. 26. Storytelling. 27. Kindling fire. 28. Body decoration. 29. Printing. 30. Musical notation. 31. The presentation of argument. 32. Photography. 33. Inducing or utilizing abstract principles. 34. Going on a vacation. 35. Construction of wheels for transportation. 36. Construction of artificial wings for flying. 37. Planning for retirement. 38. Sailing. 39. Investment. 40. Farming and ranching. 41. Mechanical engineering. 42. Transportation and use of stored power. 43. Mailing or shipping. 44. Piloting craft. 45. Recording music. 46. Inventing games. 47. Distilling alcohol. 48. Shopping. 49. Avoiding or inhibiting the spread of natural diseases. 50. Sending me provocative email.

For those of you who can't understand the argument any other way, because these other species don't have the innate ability to engage in any of these activities, all other species of animals known to mankind are inferior to us and don't have rights.

Analyze the essay:
1. Do you agree with the author that because animals do not ask for rights they should not have them? Explain.
2. Look at the author's list of fifty things animals cannot do. Do you find this compelling evidence that animals should not be given rights? Explain.

Taking Violent Action to Aid Animals Is Necessary

Laura A. Moretti

Rod Coronado is an animal rights activist who was involved in several animal rights–related organizations. He participated in many illegal actions with others from these organizations to protest harm to animals and to attempt to free them from their human captors. In 1991 he was arrested and convicted of several crimes relating to activities against fur farms and research facilities. In the following article, written after Coronado's 1999 release from prison, Laura A. Moretti interviews him about his attitudes toward animal rights and illegal activities such as those in which he participated. Coronado says that he does not regret his actions against fur farms and believes the illegal activities had an important impact.

Moretti is an animal rights activist, a writer, and a Web site designer who wrote frequently for the *Animals' Agenda*, a magazine that ceased publication in 2002.

Consider the following questions:

1. At the end of the article, Coronado says, "We *are* abolitionists." What do you think he means?
2. What does Coronado believe he achieved with his anti–fur farm actions?
3. With what organization did Coronado launch an undercover investigation of a fur farm?

Rod was hunted down like a beast on the run for his role in fur farm animal liberations—among other things. He was charged after his capture in a seven-count

Laura A. Moretti, "From Activism to Prison and Back Again—Rod Coronado," *Speaking Out for Animals: True Stories About Real People Who Rescue Animals,* edited by Kim W. Stallwood. New York: Lantern Books, 2001. Copyright © 2001 by Kim W. Stallwood. Reproduced by permission of the Institute for Animals and Society.

The militant Animal Liberation Front claimed responsibility for bombing this mink research laboratory at Michigan State University in the early 1990s.

indictment for arson and destruction of property, including one count of conspiracy and interstate racketeering.

The various charges were related to an Oregon State University (OSU) fur farm fire that burned an experimental feed building and destroyed research records; an $800,000 fire at a mink farm feed distributor that supplied OSU and dozens of other Northwest fur farms; the theft of six mink and the destruction of research at a Washington State University fur farm; a fire at an Oregon mink farm's pelt-processing building; twenty-four coyotes being rescued from a Utah State University research facility as well as destruction of its lab; and the removal of two mink and the burning of thirty-two years of mink farm research at a Michigan State University campus, all of which occurred between 1990 and 1992. . . .

With the help of Friends of Animals, Rod launched an undercover (and unprecedented) investigation of fur farm animal abuse across America, [a] grisly video of which found its way to commercial television, specifically *60 Minutes*. Never before had an unsuspecting public seen how mink were made into fur coats: the twisting of tiny heads, the broken necks, the writhing, the screaming.

"I am a warrior," Rod writes in one of his Strong Hearts publications he produced from prison. "I was unaccustomed to witnessing such cruelty without doing something about it." In an unprecedented action, Rod bought out the fur farm where he witnessed the mink killings, and then rehabilitated and released the remaining two bobcats, two lynx, and sixty mink in the Northwest wilderness. . . .

The Interview

How would you describe yourself? I consider myself an indigenous traditionalist, meaning I believe in animal rights, human rights, land rights, water rights, air rights. I respect and revere all sentient creatures. So I don't consider myself an animal rights activist or a human rights activist, because to me if you believe in the rights of one living thing, you must believe in the rights of all living things, in all of creation.

Even if it means killing some to save others? The definition of animal liberation, as it pertains to the fur farm industry, is to turn those animals back to the wilderness where they're not dependent on humans for their survival. That to me is real animal liberation. Our goal wasn't just to free those animals, but to prove to the industry and the rest of the movement that animal liberation for fur farm prisoners could actually mean returning them to the wild.

> ## Peace for All Creatures
>
> There is a war being waged, every day, against countless millions of nonhuman animals. . . . It is wishful thinking there can be 'peace' in the world if we fail to bring peace to our dealings with other animals.
>
> Tom Regan, *The Philosophy of Animal Rights*, The Culture & Animals Foundation, 1997.

In 1991 there hadn't been any fur farm liberations in the United States. We knew if such raids were ever to come, one of the biggest arguments against them would be that the animals released from the cages would cruelly starve to death in nature. . . .

The Rights of Food Animals

But what about the rights of living "food" animals? Food animals are the modern equivalent of human slaves at this period in time because their sole purpose in our reality is to fulfill human luxury. And it's very representative of our separation from nature that we allow an animal's existence to be based solely on how it can serve us. Ultimately, all food animals should be bred out of existence. They not only suffer immeasurably themselves, but the conditions they're forced to live in degrade the environment.

In the case of fur farm animals, we're talking about animals who've only been removed from the wild less than a hundred years. They are genetically identical to their wild cousins. It's one of the better causes the animals rights movement could argue for because there's no need to address the issues we face with food animals, such as what do we do with these animals once they've stopped being raised for food? On the fur farm, all we have to do is open the cages and let nature take its course. . . .

Action Breeds Results

Do you think your actions had an effect on the fur industry as a whole? Absolutely. All you have to do is look at its bottom line. They're spending more money now on security and protection from animal rights activists than they ever have. Fur farmers have to factor in the threat of an Animal Liberation Front [ALF] raid. They have to explain to their bankers how they're going to protect themselves against such threats, actions that could destabilize their income. Fur farmers today not only worry about whether they can get the fur quality from their mink, they worry whether the ALF is going to pay them a visit.

An animal rights activist in Moscow aims a gun at press photographers to protest the hunting of animals for their fur.

Demonstrators knock down a chain-link fence to protest the construction of a $14 million animal research facility at the University of California, Berkeley campus in 1990.

The posters, the bumperstickers, the demonstrations, the protests are keeping a relentless pressure on the industry, and are pushing it to the edge. What'll push them over is going to be sabotage. The industry has survived to this day because it's been able to endure the protests. That's where the ALF best serves our struggle, and it's our obligation to take full advantage of the window of opportunity they've created by continuing to put pressure on the industry, on the retail outlets, in the public eye. If we can't win the fur farm issue, we sure as hell can't win the factory farm wars.

And compromise is our struggle's enemy. We can't not say where we really come from. We can't not say we're not against all hunting. We have to be honest, and sure, we'll work on a ballot initiative to ban hound hunting in the state, but if people ask us, let's not lie, let's say we're opposed to all hunting.

It hurts our cause when people feel they're being deceived. We have to be real about that. Incremental change is fine, but when they ask us to condemn the people breaking the law, let's refuse to do so. When they ask us to accept twenty-five percent change rather than 100 percent, let's make it known to them from the start that's not what we're about.

We *are* abolitionists.

Analyze the essay:

1. Do you agree with Coronado that breaking the law is permissible to end something you believe is wrong, or do you think it is better to work to make changes through the law? Explain.
2. Some other famous lawbreakers for a cause are Henry David Thoreau, Mahatma Gandhi, and Rosa Parks. Look up one of these people, then compare their actions to Coronado's.

Animal Rights Terrorism Must Stop

Wesley J. Smith

Animal rights organizations often have entertaining publicity campaigns to convince people to agree with their point of view. But, says Wesley J. Smith, some of these organizations are now turning "to the dark side"—using violence and lawbreaking to make their point. These extremists have used threats and violence to inhibit the work of animal research labs. Some of them are even designated as terrorists by the government. Nearly as bad, says Smith, are the mainstream animal rights organizations that are openly or secretly supporting the extremists. He believes these animal rights extremists must be stopped.

Smith is a senior fellow at the Discovery Institute (a Washington, D.C.– and Seattle-based think tank), an attorney, and the author of books on cloning, euthanasia, and other topics.

Consider the following questions:

1. According to the author, what have animal rights terrorists done to harm the British drug-testing facility Huntingdon Life Sciences?
2. What does the author mean when he says that "the firewall that groups such as PETA have long maintained between themselves and ARL [animal rights/liberation] terrorists seems to be breaking down"?
3. What evidence of terrorist intentions does the author provide from the Animal Liberation Front's own Web site?

Wesley J. Smith, "Terrorists, Too: Exposing Animal-Rights Terrorism," www.national review.com, October 2, 2002. Copyright © 2002 by the National Review, Inc. Reproduced by permission of United Feature Syndicate, Inc.

The animal-rights/liberation (ARL) movement isn't funny anymore. Unable to get most of society to agree that animals are the moral equals of people or that farming pigs is akin to holding human slaves, some ARL activists have crossed to the dark side—animal-rights terrorism. Indeed, violence, vandalism, and personal threats from groups such as the Animal Liberation Front (ALF), the Earth Liberation Front (ELF), and Stop Huntingdon Animal Cruelty (SHAC) have ratcheted up so radically against medical researchers, ranchers, and others in recent years, that animal-rights terrorism is now being scrutinized by one of the most respected antiterrorist organizations in the world, the Southern Poverty Law Center (SPLC).

You have to be especially dangerous and potentially violent to warrant attention from the SPLC. Cofounded by renowned civil-rights attorney Morris Dees, the group is best known for its successful legal struggle against hate

A police officer in full riot gear subdues an animal rights activist demonstrating against Huntingdon Life Sciences, a products-testing company that routinely conducts animal experimentation.

groups such as the Ku Klux Klan [KKK] and Aryan Nation. One of the center's most useful projects is the respected *SPLC Intelligence Report (IR)*, a quarterly magazine that offers in-depth analysis of political extremism in the United States. The Fall 2002 *IR* exposes the depth of the threat of ARL terrorism—earning ALF, ELF, and SHAC a level of infamy usually reserved for American extremist groups such as the KKK, Aryan Nation, and the American Nazi party.

Threats and Violence

According to the *IR* exposé, "From Push to Shove," ARL terrorists such as ALF and SHAC regularly employ "death threats, fire bombings, and violent assaults" against those they accuse of abusing animals. Some of the cruelest attacks have been mounted by SHAC against executives for Huntingdon Life Sciences, a British drug-testing facil-

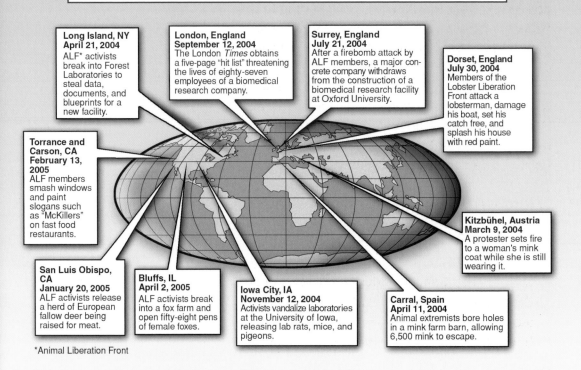

Acts of Violence Committed for Animal Rights

**Long Island, NY
April 21, 2004**
ALF* activists break into Forest Laboratories to steal data, documents, and blueprints for a new facility.

**London, England
September 12, 2004**
The London *Times* obtains a five-page "hit list" threatening the lives of eighty-seven employees of a biomedical research company.

**Surrey, England
July 21, 2004**
After a firebomb attack by ALF members, a major concrete company withdraws from the construction of a biomedical research facility at Oxford University.

**Dorset, England
July 30, 2004**
Members of the Lobster Liberation Front attack a lobsterman, damage his boat, set his catch free, and splash his house with red paint.

**Torrance and Carson, CA
February 13, 2005**
ALF members smash windows and paint slogans such as "McKillers" on fast food restaurants.

**Kitzbühel, Austria
March 9, 2004**
A protester sets fire to a woman's mink coat while she is still wearing it.

**San Luis Obispo, CA
January 20, 2005**
ALF activists release a herd of European fallow deer being raised for meat.

**Bluffs, IL
April 2, 2005**
ALF activists break into a fox farm and open fifty-eight pens of female foxes.

**Iowa City, IA
November 12, 2004**
Activists vandalize laboratories at the University of Iowa, releasing lab rats, mice, and pigeons.

**Carral, Spain
April 11, 2004**
Animal extremists bore holes in a mink farm barn, allowing 6,500 mink to escape.

*Animal Liberation Front

Source: National Animal Interest Alliance, http://naiaonline.org.

ity that uses animals to test drugs for safety before they are tested on people. Indeed, the threats and violence became so extreme that Huntingdon fled Britain out of the fear that some of their own were going to be killed. They had good cause: The company's managing director was badly beaten by three masked assailants swinging baseball bats, while another executive was temporarily blinded with a caustic substance sprayed into his eyes. . . .

The deafening lack of condemnation by mainstream ARL organizations against these terrorist tactics speaks louder than their oft-stated claims to being a peaceful social movement. Indeed, the firewall that groups such as PETA have long maintained between themselves and ARL terrorists seems to be breaking down. PETA's tax-exempt status is being challenged because it admittedly paid $1,500 to ELF. (According to the FBI, ELF is one of the nation's largest terrorist groups.) According to the SPLC, PETA also provided funds to convicted animal- or environmental-rights terrorists. . . .

The *Intelligence Report* also reveals that known ELF and ALF activists are routinely invited to speak at the yearly Washington, D.C., animal-rights conference sponsored by PETA and the Humane Society of the United States. Further, the *IR* quotes PETA's Bruce Friedrich as stating:

> If we really believe that animals have the same right to be free from pain and suffering at our hands, then of course we're going to be blowing things up and smashing windows. . . . I think it's a great way to bring animal liberation, considering the level of suffering, the atrocities. I think it would be great if all of the fast-food outlets, slaughterhouses, these laboratories, and banks that fund them, exploded tomorrow.

The Damage Done

America's present environmental and animal-rights terrorists have committed arsons, assaults, vandalism on a massive scale, and a host of other property crimes that cripple food producers and resource providers.

Richard B. Berman, testimony before the U.S. House of Representatives, Committee on Resources, February 12, 2002.

After repeated threats by animal rights activists against executives of Huntingdon Life Sciences, the company closed its London office.

Inciting Terrorism

PETA should be roundly condemned for permitting one of its own to advocate violence and for associating with violent groups such as ALF. In this regard, it is worth pointing out that ALF has gone so far down the terrorist path that it posted a how-to-commit-arson manual on its website. Called "Arson Around With Auntie ALF," the tract promotes the use of incendiaries to destroy animal "abusing" facilities because "pound for pound" they "can do more damage than explosives against many types of targets." There is a downside, however, which ARL terrorists are advised to consider when deciding how to best carry out their planned attacks. During the "time lag" between the setting of the fire and "the destruction of the target," *Arson Around* warns, the "fire may be discovered and controlled or put out." Thus, even though it may do less damage, the upside of explosives is that "once detonated, [the explosion] has done its work."

Unlike hierarchical terrorist organizations such as al Qaeda that keeps close control over operations, the ALF terrorist manual urges its minions to adopt an anarchist approach. They are to join together in small cells of two or three people and *never* tell anyone about their ALF affiliation. When they carry out their assaults, they are instructed to spray-paint animal-rights slogans signed by "ALF" all over the crime scenes before fleeing. In that way, it will be all but impossible for law enforcement to infiltrate the terrorist cells or solve the crimes. Best of all, ALF will get the credit for the terror attack but its known organizers will honestly be able to claim that they had no foreknowledge of the plan or who actually carried out the attack.

Going Downhill

Where do we go from here? Downhill, apparently. The *SPLC Intelligence Report* worries that "further violence seems almost inevitable" as animal-rights terrorist leaders inspire "a new breed of activist." Sooner or later, someone is likely to be killed.

This isn't alarmist rhetoric. In the Netherlands, an animal-rights extremist allegedly assassinated a candidate for parliament, perhaps because he defended pig farming in a debate with animal-rights activists. An ELF representative recently suggested that it might be time to "take up the gun," while the *Intelligence Report* quotes Kevin Jonas of SHAC-USA as personalizing JFK's famous quote, "If you make peaceful revolution impossible, you make violent revolution inevitable."

Analyze the essay:

1. The author cites a quotation from President John F. Kennedy: "If you make peaceful revolution impossible, you make violent revolution inevitable." What do you think this quote means? How would peaceful revolution be made impossible?

2. Do you agree with the author that the animal rights extremists he describes should be classified as terrorists? Explain.

Animals Must Be Used in Medical Research

Ellen Frankel Paul

We need to continue using animals in medical research, according to Ellen Frankel Paul, the author of the following article. She states that animal experimentation (also called vivisection) has been responsible for many medical advances that save millions of human lives today. It is the most promising source of a cure for spinal cord injuries, and it has been responsible for such important developments as the polio vaccine, the ability to transplant organs, and many other medical marvels. Paul points out that the use of animals in medical research has greatly decreased in recent years but that it is still essential.

Paul is a professor of political science and philosophy at Bowling Green State University in Ohio. She has written several books, including *Why Animal Experimentation Matters: The Use of Animals in Medical Research*.

Consider the following questions:

1. According to the author, why do most people in advanced industrial societies have trouble with the idea of animal testing?
2. Does Paul believe that alternatives to animal-based research can produce the same kind of medical progress? Explain.
3. List five examples of medical advances the author says would not have been possible without animal experimentation.

A teenager is rushed from an after-prom party to the nearest emergency room with head and neck trauma from a diving board accident. His neck is broken, and the

Ellen Frankel Paul, "Why Animal Experimentation Matters," *Society*, vol. 39, September/October 2002, pp. 7–15. Copyright © 2002 by Transaction Publishers. Reproduced by permission of Copyright Clearance Center, Inc.

prognosis is grim. The youngster will in all likelihood be a quadriplegic, with little prospect of ever recovering the use of his limbs. . . .

Where does hope lie for this teenager and for those who will surely follow him? Cutting-edge research on regenerating damaged nerves may one day unlock the secret, and ER [emergency room] doctors will then be able to offer many of these victims a brighter future than a life of severe impairment of major bodily functions. . . . However, as in all things scientific, the whole process is highly speculative, and many promising beginnings in spinal cord regeneration have led down blind alleys. While nerves in other parts of the body do repair themselves, spinal cord and brain research is aimed at unlocking one of the human body's most mysterious defense systems.

An AIDS researcher holds a lab mouse with a transplanted human immune system. Studies with such mice have yielded significant information about the immune system.

Animals Used in Medical Experiments

Frogs

The nerve endings in the skin of many frogs produce antibiotic substances that fight infections and make wounds heal more quickly.

Squids

Squids have large, simple cells and organs that help scientists learn about basic biological processes.

Horseshoe Crabs

Horseshoe crabs are used for vision studies because their eyes are similar to the human eye.

Snakes

The venom from certain poisonous snakes contains a chemical that helps prevent high blood pressure in humans.

Rodents

Rodents are used to study cancer, hypertension, nerve and spinal injury, nutrition, the brain, and much more.

Source: Federation of American Societies for Experimental Biology, www.faseb.org/opar/poster/a_page.html#six_animals.

Medical Progress Through Animal Experiments

Breakthroughs in treating spinal cord injuries, like practically all medical advances, depend upon experimentation on animals. . . .

Although the case for animal experimentation is a strong one, animal rights advocates have thus far been much more successful in stating their case to the public. Most people in advanced industrial societies have little contact with animals for most are generations removed from the farm. Animals are our furry children, spoiled and doted upon as our beloved pets. The slaughter of farm animals is not within our repertoire. It is very easy, then, for animal rights activists to tug at our emotions with pictures of laboratory cats and dogs suffering the aftereffects of disfiguring surgeries. It is difficult for us to think of medical advances and the furtherance of human knowledge when we imagine the visage of our family pet on the laboratory animal's body.

Despite the claims to the contrary by animal rights activists, for most vital medical research there is at this time no sufficient substitute for animals. A ban on experimentation—or the implementation of a vastly more restrictive regime than the one that the government presently enforces—would leave the population vulnerable to the next deadly AIDS or Ebola virus that suddenly appears. Antibiotics that are now nearing the end of their utility in combating many deadly bacteria could not be replaced by next-generation drugs of greater efficacy. People afflicted with genetic or communicable diseases, or suffering from catastrophic accidents, would be denied hope of future discoveries that might palliate or remedy their afflictions. Life does not stand still, and neither do the threats to human life in the form of pathogens as yet unknown. We ought not hobble our ingenious, dedicated, and compassionate research scientists who want to advance human knowledge so that future threats to life, organic and otherwise, are manageable, rather than mysterious and calamitous.

The Contribution of Animals to Human Health

A perusal of the list of research projects that have received the Nobel Prize in medicine since its inception in 1901 reveals just how critical animal experimentation has been to the understanding of biological functions, pathogens, genetic diseases, and their treatment. Mice and other rodents contributed to the 1984 recipients' development of the technique of forming monoclonal antibodies, a discovery that led to new tools for fighting some types of cancers.

The Importance of Animal Research

We cannot think of an area of medical research that does not owe many of its most important advances to animal experiments.

Jack H. Botting and Adrian R. Morrison, "Animal Research Is Vital to Medicine," *Scientific American*, February 1, 1997.

Mice also played a part in the 1996 winner's understanding of how the immune system detects cells infected with viruses. Earlier, mice were instrumental in the understanding of penicillin's role in fighting bacterial infections, a contribution that garnered a Nobel Prize in 1945. Perhaps most memorably, mice contributed to the development of the vaccine that eradicated polio. Cows and sheep were the subjects of experiments that led to the 1905 prize for discoveries involving the pathogenesis of tuberculosis, while work with pigeons led to a 1902 award for unraveling the life cycle of malaria. Antibiotics depended for their development, and still do, on animal experimentation, with the 1952 prize for the discovery of streptomycin as one example of how the guinea pig advanced the treatment of infectious diseases. The recipient in 1964 experimented on rats to understand how our bodies metabolize cholesterol and other fats that clog our arteries and lead to heart attacks, strokes, and coronary diseases that shorten the lives of millions and leave others in a debilitated condition. Dogs and cats made immensely useful contributions of their own: organ transplantation techniques developed in dogs garnered a Nobel Prize in 1990, and work on dogs also contributed to the 1924 prize winner's development of the electrocardiogram, which has become the routine screening device for cardiovascular disease. Cats aided our understanding of how nerve transmitters function (the subject of the 1970 prize), how visual information is stored in the brain (1981), and how the brain organizes itself to coordinate internal organs of the body (1949).

Animals Are Our Best Hope

For the foreseeable future, then, animals as research subjects are our best hope for understanding and combating incapacitating or deadly human diseases and conditions. Treatments for AIDS, diabetes, and toxoplasmosis; organ

A rhesus monkey undergoes surgery on its jaw in Sichuan University Hospital in China to test new techniques for human facial plastic surgery.

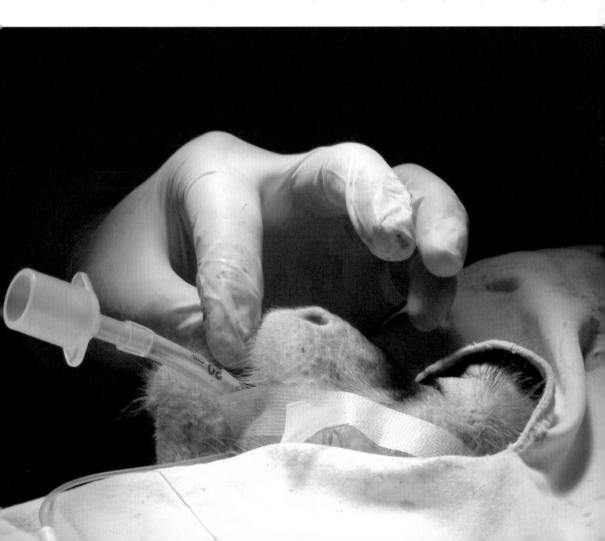

transplants; the training of emergency room physicians in trauma techniques; life-saving heart and lung surgeries; the study of neurological diseases such as amyotrophic lateral sclerosis (ALS or Lou Gehrig's disease); the study of gene therapies to fight cancer—these and countless other methods of treating diseases and educating medical personnel depend upon experimentation on animals. Most of the time, these goals simply require the use of rodents, but sometimes, out of necessity, higher animals must be used as well.

Analyze the essay:

1. The author of this viewpoint believes it is acceptable to experiment on animals if it will result in the betterment of humankind. What is your take on this idea? Do you agree or disagree? Explain your reasoning.

2. One persuasive technique the author uses in her essay is to recount the numerous diseases that have been cured or treated through animal experimentation. In your opinion, is this technique effective? What is your opinion of animal experimentation after being exposed to the author's list of things it has helped science accomplish?

Animal-Based Research Should End

Gail Gorman

Animal-based research (vivisection) to discover medical
knowledge and cures has been practiced for centuries.
According to Gail Gorman, author of the following article, it is time to stop this outdated practice. According to
Gorman, all of the millions of experiments that have been
done have resulted in many failures. In addition, there are
numerous dissimilarities between animals and humans
that cause misleading experimental results. Gorman suggests that this inadequate research be abandoned in favor
of more modern research techniques.

Gorman is an author and entrepreneur who writes frequently for *Nutrition Health Review: The Consumer's Medical
Journal*.

Consider the following questions:

1. According to the author, what might have happened if Alexander Fleming had relied heavily on animal testing?
2. What are five examples of how animals react
   to drugs differently than humans, according
   to Gorman?
3. What are three alternatives to animal experimentation that the author describes?

Known as vivisection, or sometimes as animal modeling, using animals to understand humans is still
the weapon of choice for fighting our most entrenched
diseases; for deciding federal regulation of potentially
hazardous materials, including new prescription drugs;

Gail Gorman, "Congratulations, Madame, the Rabbit Is Dead," *Nutrition Health Review:
The Consumer's Medical Journal*, 2003, p. 2. Copyright © 2003 by the *Nutrition Health
Review: The Consumer's Medical Journal*. Reproduced by permission.

*Animal rights
activists outside the
Harvard University
primate research
center condemn the
center's use of
primates to conduct
research on infectious
diseases.*

and even for teaching surgical methods. Yes, many doctors may have received their medical school training by practicing on dogs.

The question is, does the sacrifice lead to the save? What is the efficacy (and the sanity) of allowing a 2,000-year-old practice to dominate in the face of more advanced and potentially more accurate options? . . .

Is Animal Testing Effective?

In truth, animal testing is still the predominant method for deciding what is good or bad for humans, especially when it comes to prescription medicines and other potentially hazardous substances. Surely, if this is the principal method, it has proved to be the best. However, a growing number of doctors and scientists are vehemently refuting the claim. For example:

- Of 25 drugs found useful in treating stroke in animals over the past 10 years, not one has proved effective in clinical practice.

- A therapeutic dose of aspirin in a human is poisonous to cats, has no effect on fever in horses, and causes birth defects in rats, cats, dogs, guinea pigs and monkeys, yet is considered safe for pregnant women.
- Benzene causes leukemia in humans but not in mice.
- Insulin produces birth defects in animals but not in humans.
- Cortisone produces birth defects in mice but not in people.
- Morphine calms people but excites cats, goats, and horses.
- The antibiotic chloramphenicol produces aplastic anemia in some humans, but it saves animals.
- The arthritis drug fenclozic acid causes liver toxicity in people but not in rats, mice, dogs, monkeys, rabbits, guinea pigs, ferrets, cats, pigs, or horses.
- Penicillin is highly poisonous to guinea pigs and hamsters. If [British bacteriologist] Alexander Fleming had relied heavily on animal testing in 1928, he might have dismissed the drug altogether as too dangerous.

The issue, scientists and medical professionals tell us, is that there is ambiguity in animal testing. For example, tamoxifen, which is used to treat women who have had breast cancer because it reduces the incidence of mammary cancer in rodents, actually increases the incidence of liver cancer in rodents and appears to be nephrotoxic (injurious to the kidneys).

Individual Species Have Unique Genetic Makeups

For many years, arsenic was not banned as a human carcinogen. It took scientists until 1980 to induce arsenic-based cancer in animals. Yet metallurgical and other industry workers were contracting cancer after repeated contact, causing doctors to suggest arsenic as a carcinogen as much as 180 years earlier.

Any school child knows that each individual species has unique genetic makeup. When it comes to comparing

'Now that you've all had a chance to try the shampoo, we would like you to fill in this questionnaire.'

NAF. © 2001 by *The Spectator*. Reproduced by permission.

humans with animals, one must consider massive variations in histology (structure, composition, and function of tissues), biochemistry (chemistry of living organisms), morphology (structure of organisms), physiology (function of living organisms), and other species characteristics. Even something as simple as metabolism or absorption rates can cause great variation among different species.

It only follows, then, that many human diseases simply cannot be replicated in the animal world. In fact, most research must first find a way to induce the disease because it does not occur in the animal naturally. The causative organisms of pneumonia, for example, are not generally harmful to laboratory animals.

Research on human cholera has repeatedly failed to reproduce the disease in animals. Robert Koch, who isolated the germ and subsequently described how it was transmitted, relied solely on clinical observation to do so.

Unsuccessful attempts to induce liver cirrhosis through the consumption of alcohol delayed recognition of the connection for years, despite overwhelming clinical evidence to the contrary. The same is true of asbestos-induced lung cancer and radiation links to childhood leukemia.

Unsuccessful attempts to induce lung cancer in laboratory animals delayed health warnings for 16 years, even though evidence in humans linked it to cigarette smoking. . . .

Alternatives to Animal Experimentation

We see that vivisection has its faults. What are the alternatives?

In fact, a number of organizations are actively calling for "the three Rs":

- Refinement: better animal handling techniques in order to reduce the pain and suffering of the animal.
- Reduction: better knowledge management so that fewer animals need to be used.
- Replacement: the use of updated tools.

Information is the key. Access to information can prevent unnecessary duplication of animal work. Unfortunately, much of the data is considered of commercial significance and therefore cannot always be found in the public domain.

In vitro ("in glass") techniques are available to test against human tissue in test tubes or outside the living organism.

To determine safe levels of pollutants, a researcher administers small doses of contaminants to a paid volunteer at the Rancho Los Amigos National Rehabilitation Center in California.

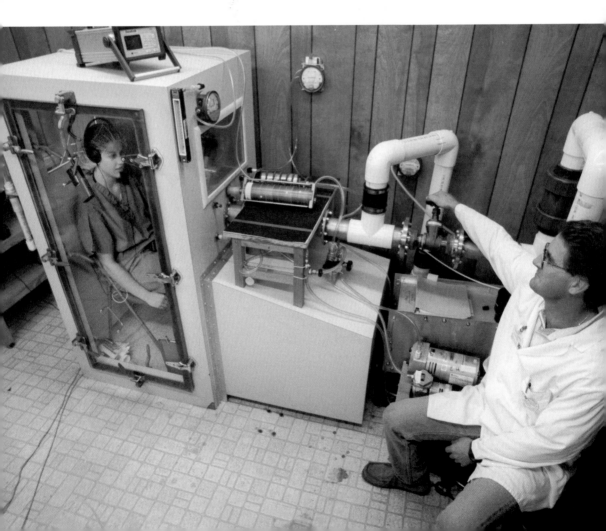

In silico, the use of computer-based modeling systems, has already begun to take hold in training situations. Physiologically based pharmacokinetic modeling predicts the disposition of a chemical and its metabolites by integrating species-specific physiological parameters with partition coefficients for chemical and metabolic constants already known from in vivo (live) tests.

Physicochemical techniques use existing data in combination with structure-activity relationships to predict the likely biological effects of chemicals.

Finally, with due consideration to moral and safety issues, the clinical trial [testing on humans] is still the best method for predicting what a substance will do in a human host. Of course, one must be sure that all of the other preclinical techniques have been adhered to. Is that not precisely what we are doing now, only with animals as our preclinical predictors?

If there are alternatives that are at least as accurate, why do we still rely so heavily on hapless rabbits? Vivisection is medicine from the days when the world was flat. Is it not time to move on?

Analyze the essay:

1. After reading this viewpoint, consider whether your school uses animals in any of its science classes. If so, how are the animals used? What do you think of this practice? Explain.

2. In this viewpoint the author argues against animal testing. In the previous viewpoint the author argues in favor of such practice. After reading both viewpoints, what is your opinion on animal testing? Explain your reasoning.

The Fur Industry Continues to Harm Animals

Viewpoint

Seven

Danielle Bays and Lydia Nichols

Animal rights activists protest the production, buying, and wearing of fur coats. They argue that the animals that are farmed to produce furs are treated inhumanely. The fur industry has long contended that these protests have resulted in poor sales and reduced production. According to Danielle Bays and Lydia Nichols, authors of the following article, while fewer fur coats are produced, the fur industry produces massive amounts of fur trim. This trim is used on collars for coats, jackets, and sweaters. Thus, the inhumane trapping and farming of fur-bearing animals continues. The authors caution that by placing an emphasis on fur trim and making it available even in discount stores, the fur industry is seducing consumers into believing that wearing only a little fur is not bad.

Consider the following questions:

1. According to the authors, how do trapped animals suffer differently than those on fur farms?
2. List three evils of fur farms, as cited by the authors.
3. Why might fur trim become more profitable to fur producers than full-length fur coats, according to Bays and Nichols?

When you think of fur "fashion" you might picture a traditional mink coat or maybe even a more contemporary, brightly colored fox-fur chubby. But what about a microfiber jacket trimmed with fox fur? Although

Danielle Bays and Lydia Nichols, "The Fur Fringe," *The Animals' Agenda*, October 12, 2001. Copyright © 2001 by The Animal Rights Network. Reproduced by permission of the Institute for Animals and Society.

historically the fur industry's emphasis has been on full-length coats, fur trim is becoming a mainstay of the trade. . . .

A Little Trim, a Lot of Suffering

For some people, wearing a garment with "just a little" fur trim may not seem as inhumane as wearing a full-length fur. But the animals suffer and die just the same, victims of the institutionalized cruelty of fur farms or the agony of steel traps.

Foxes are the most common animals used for fur trim. Ninety percent of the foxes raised on fur farms are killed for the fur-trim market. Blue foxes (the industry term for cage-raised arctic foxes) are the primary type used, followed by the silver fox (cage-raised red foxes). Trapped foxes—red, gray, and arctic—are also skinned for the trim trade.

Mink and sable—both those raised on intensive farms and those trapped in the wild—are regularly converted into neckpieces and other vanity accessories. Male mink, whose pelts are larger, are killed almost exclusively for trim (makers of full-length coats prefer female pelts). Other animals regularly exploited for the trim trade include such wild-caught animals as raccoons, coyotes, and beavers, as well as cage-raised chinchillas and Finraccoons (the moniker given to raccoon dogs, a wild Asian species commonly raised on Finnish fur farms).

Inhumane Fur Farms

Despite the benign-sounding industry propaganda surrounding fur "ranches," there is nothing humane about fur farms. Life inside small, barren wire cages is a far cry from these animals' natural environments. The animals often resort to unnatural behaviors, such as incessant pacing, self-mutilation, and even cannibalism, to escape the boredom and frustration created by their harsh and deprived conditions. Foxes are extremely fearful of humans; they tremble, defecate, and withdraw to the rear of their cages when approached. They have a high rate of

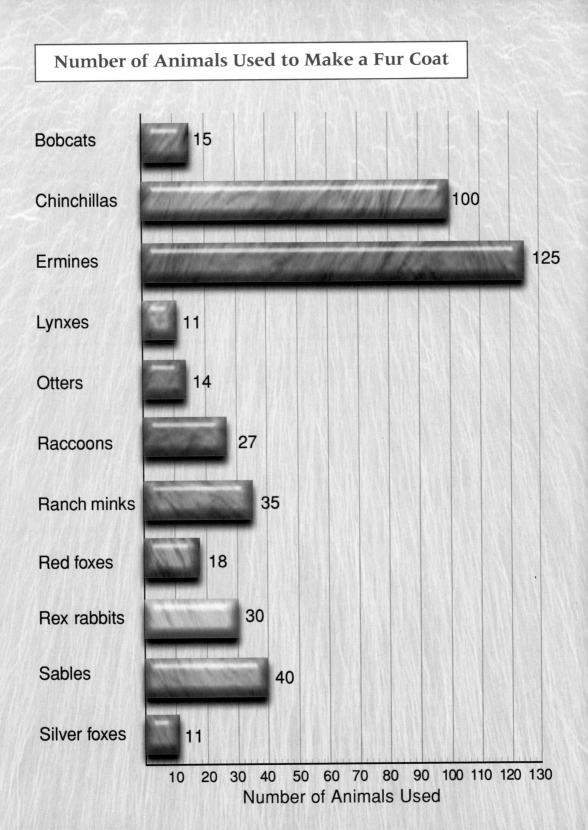

Number of Animals Used to Make a Fur Coat

Animal	Number of Animals Used
Bobcats	15
Chinchillas	100
Ermines	125
Lynxes	11
Otters	14
Raccoons	27
Ranch minks	35
Red foxes	18
Rex rabbits	30
Sables	40
Silver foxes	11

Number of Animals Used

Source: Animal Protection Institute, www.api4animals.org.

cannibalism—primarily mothers killing their young—as a result of cramped caging. Fox farmers lose an estimated 20 percent of their animals prematurely, and half of those deaths result from cannibalism. Death is no easy escape either, as the most common killing method of farmed foxes is anal electrocution.

The increased use of raccoon fur as trim on cloth and leather garments has renewed demand for this type of fur. The number of raccoons trapped in the United States dropped an estimated 75 percent this past [2000–2001] season, but with the trim market expanding, the forecast for this winter may be deadly for raccoons.

Trapped animals suffer a different type of torture than those on fur farms. Volumes of documentation prove that

Fur-clad members of the activist group, People for Ethical Treatment of Animals (PETA), sit in cages in New Hampshire to protest the treatment of animals on fur farms.

leghold traps mutilate wild animals caught in their grip—ripping flesh, tearing tendons and ligaments, and even breaking bones. Many animals, especially raccoons, will chew or twist off their own limbs in a desperate attempt to escape. The indiscriminate nature of all traps is well documented, with scores of nontarget animals (including family companions) caught by traps intended for other animals. Body-gripping traps often cause excruciating pain and prolonged death; neck snares are particularly cruel for coyotes and foxes because the significant musculature around these animals' tracheas and carotid arteries slows death and magnifies suffering.

Buyer Beware

By actively marketing fur-trimmed items, the fur industry seeks to inundate consumers with fur-buying options. Shoppers don't have to go to fur salons or seek out furriers anymore; fur trim can be found even in discount stores, where, ironically, people may assume the trim is therefore synthetic. Consumers are looking for innovative apparel rather than the traditional styles of fur fashion, one reason why the fur industry markets fur-trim products to a younger generation in an effort to broaden their customer base.

The fur industry views fur trim as a consumer's "introduction" to fur: something that will make a person want to purchase a more expensive full-fur coat in the future. This is simply a desperate marketing scheme to raise interest in a dying fashion. Consumers may be able to justify fur trim by accepting false notions of its origin, yet the leap to a full-fur item could well be dismissed as too much animal suffering or as an ostentatious fashion "don't."

According to fur industry publications, furriers believe fur-trimmed garments will become more important than all-fur garments in terms of repeat business because such items might be replaced in only a few years, whereas a fur coat may last for 20 years or more. Furriers also believe that fur trim is what helped bring younger consumers back to fur stores and boutiques. Additionally, they believe these consumers are much more receptive to fur than they were five years ago. Designers such as Gucci, Chanel, and Christian Dior are using more vibrant colors and unique styles in hopes of attracting younger consumers.

People who check garment labels can be confused or even deceived by the fact that most products aren't required to state whether trim is made of real fur or what kind of animal was killed to produce it. With fur trim coming in such a range of colors and cuts, it has become increasingly difficult for consumers to identify what is real and what is not. Labels don't help much, since labels on most trimmed products aren't required to state whether the fur is real and, if it is, what kind of animal was killed to obtain it. A loophole in the federal Fur Products Labeling Act exempts garments costing less than $150 from truth-in-labeling provisions.

As a movement [focused on preventing cruelty to animals], we must broaden our focus on the fur industry to include fur trim and to condemn this trend as vigorously as we do full-fur items. We can't let someone off the ethical hook because they are wearing "just a little" fur. Let's educate the public about the trim trade and the cruelty that is inherent in each and every collar and cuff.

Analyze the essay:

The authors of this viewpoint reject the use of any fur products in clothing. What do you think—is wearing "just a little" fur, such as a fur collar, permissible? Explain your answer.

The Fur Industry Is Environmentally Friendly

Teresa Platt and Simon Ward

Authors Teresa Platt and Simon Ward are pleased that fur is becoming popular once again. Platt and Ward point out the inconsistent practices of some fashion designers who claim that they will not use fur in their designs, but then use shearling, which is a kind of fur. They also point out that using fur and leather is beneficial to society in many ways: It helps the environment by keeping the waste from meat animals such as cows and sheep out of landfills, and it allows farmers to make a living raising livestock, which is often difficult. Fur-bearing animals also do their part for the environment by eating the additional waste from meat animals. The authors conclude that the fur industry not only provides a beautiful, luxurious product but also provides many useful services to society.

Platt is the executive director of the Fur Commission USA (FCUSA), an organization that promotes the fur industry. Ward is FCUSA's Web master.

Consider the following questions:

1. What conflict do the authors see in designer Stella McCartney producing designs that combine shearling and faux fur?
2. Do Platt and Ward seem to think there is any difference between using shearling or chinchilla?
3. How do the authors say fur-bearing animals such as domesticated (farmed) fox and mink help the environment?

Teresa Platt and Simon Ward, "Producers, Consumers, and Clothing Confusion," *Fur Farm Letter,* December 2000. Copyright © 2000 by the Fur Commission USA. Reproduced by permission.

A fashion model sports a bleached silver fox coat during a showing of the fall 2005 clothing line of actress Jennifer Lopez.

As the new millennium dawned [in 2000], a stampede began. With fashion designers, writers and other trend-setters cracking the whip, a herd of leathers, suedes, shear-lings and furs charged down the catwalks of America and Europe, and straight out the doors of trendy boutiques. One year later, the stampede continues unabated, but how far have the consumers who buy these creations come in terms of understanding animal-based clothing, and in par-ticular fur?

Without doubt, the stigma of political incorrectness that surrounded fur during the 1990s is fading, but before it can be laid forever to rest, there's some mud-dled thinking that needs to be cleared up.

Why Faux Fur?

"Shearlings will be particularly popular," predicted one writer last March [2000], after viewing a [fashion] collec-tion from [designer] Stella McCartney featuring "shear-ling with faux fur for Chloe."

Shearling with faux fur? If ever there were a combina-tion that epitomized society's confusion over wearing ani-mal hides, shearling and faux fur could be it!

Shearling is not wool. It is sheepskin—the pelt of a sheep that has been killed to satisfy a human need. And since it still has all those long hairs attached, it is, in fact, sheep's fur.

Faux fur, in contrast, is a petrochemical political state-ment. It imitates the pelts of animals with long hairs attached, but no animal or other organism was directly killed to produce it.

So what does this half-organic, half-synthetic creation say about the designer, and what message does it convey to consumers? McCartney has done *pro bono* work for People for the Ethical Treatment of Animals (PETA), and is the designer of choice for many fellow vegetarians, so some people take her selection of materials seriously.

Says McCartney, "I try not to work in leather too much, because I'm a vegetarian."

But the fact remains that she *does* use leather, which is simply a cow's pelt with the hair removed, and she *does* use a sheep's pelt with the hair still attached. So what's the deal with the faux fur?

Waste Not, Want Not

McCartney's confusion is based on the erroneous idea that the production of fur from carnivores is separate and distinct from human food production, and therefore "unnecessary." Leather and shearling, by contrast, she sees merely as "by-products" of human food production. Thus, even though they are not necessary in themselves, they should not be wasted—or so the thinking goes.

Meat-eaters can feel good about wearing leather, right? Since we've already eaten its muscles and a few internal organs, what could be wrong with wrapping its hairless hide around our feet and shoulders? Waste not, want not. . . .

Leftovers

The first question we should ask is: what happened to all the parts of the slaughtered sheep that *didn't* end up in our wardrobes or on the end of our forks? If making use of the hide that dinner came wrapped in makes us feel good, shouldn't we also care about what happened to the rest of the animal—the head, legs, hooves, entrails, tail, bones, and nether regions?

Landfills are an obvious and unacceptable option for these "leftovers." In many countries, our pet dogs and cats are the principal scavengers beneath our dinner tables. In some countries, leftovers are fed to pigs and chickens, or used as organic fertilizer for crops.

The Benefits of Fur

All of society benefits from well regulated hunting and trapping. These activities help to ensure stable and healthy wildlife populations, and reduce the risks of damage to property, while providing useful products for people. Fur is a renewable, natural resource.

Department of Environment and Wildlife, Government of Quebec.

Wilkinson. © by the Cartoonists and Writers Syndicate. Reproduced by permission.

In fur-farming countries, there's another option: feeding a good percentage of these animal remains to domesticated carnivores [such as farmed mink and fox], thereby producing another level of products for human use.

By cleaning up the scraps from our dinner table, domesticated mink and fox form an integral part of the human food-production chain. They live off the remains of Bessy the Cow after she's given her all producing milk, or the steer raised for his prime steak, or the sheep and goats raised for food, fiber or both. Add in all the leftovers from fish production, and expired eggs and cheese, and you can imagine how rich a diet can be for carnivores living among us.

An average farmed mink consumes 20 times its body weight annually, while a fox consumes 30 times, transforming all these parts of grazers that humans won't touch

Sheep shearers remove the wool from sheep in Victoria, Australia. In addition to their wool, sheep farmers depend on their animals' pelts and meat for their livelihood.

into a valuable product. Next time you see a beautiful, full-length mink coat, try seeing it instead as 2.5 tons of recycled waste that won't be clogging up landfills. And in addition to the fur pelts, the carcasses of these carnivores yield secondary products and by-products such as mink oil, protein meal, and ingredients for cosmetics, paints, tires and glue, while their feces are used for organic fertilizer.

Primary, Secondary, and By-products

The second concept we must grasp is how a farmer makes a living by selling primary and secondary products, and how the value of by-products made from "leftovers" can reduce operating costs and make farming a little more profitable. . . .

Secondary products such as leather in the beef industry or mutton in the wool industry make an important contribution to farmers' financial viability. And, depending on market conditions, today's secondary product may be tomorrow's primary product. Ban a secondary product and a farmer is going to be financially hurt. Or remove production sectors such as fur farming, which take sheep and cattle farmers' "waste" and transform it into a primary product, and those farmers will incur new disposal costs, while the waste will go to landfills.

Indeed, all sheep and cattle farmers breed their animals for one primary product which brings the best market price, plus one or more secondary products. A dairy farmer may pay his mortgage supplying milk to cheese or yoghurt producers, but when members of his herd are spent, secondary products such as hides bring in a little extra. This farmer, and every farmer, will also have need of a company that will take the "leftovers" and maximize their value by turning them into other products. . . .

Abandoning the Contradictions, Embracing the Utilitarian

The reality is that the world has few gentleman farmers, such as Stella McCartney's father Paul, who keeps sheep just for their aesthetic value. Most farmers and consumers enjoy the beauty of sheep on the hillsides but also appreciate their utilitarian values—their wool, pelt and meat— in feeding and clothing us.

Let's hope next season the fashion writers and consumers look at the animal-based products on the runways with new respect. Let's hope they see the beautiful animals behind the exquisite products and abandon the contradictions, embracing the utilitarian.

Take a long look and appreciate the fruits of the labors of those folk who feed and clothe us: suede and leather from cattle bred primarily for beef and dairy products; sheepskin, felt and wools from the Karakul, Merino and Awassi. And don't forget the lowly goat: mohair from Angora, and fine cashmere wools from the Cashmere and Zhongwei breeds.

And there on the runways, stalking the grazers, will be the magnificent carnivores bred on a diet rich from the "leftovers": mink in pearl, mahogany and black, blue iris, sapphire, violet and more; fox in silver, fawn, platinum, amazing reds and more.

It's a stampede on the runways and walkways of this Earth with animals, in all their diverse forms, giving us sustenance and keeping us warm and fashionable.

Analyze the essay:

1. Faux fur and many other synthetic materials are petrochemical products—they are made from petroleum. The authors note that faux fur is "a petrochemical political statement." What do you think they mean?
2. Do you agree that supporting the fur industry helps the environment? Explain.

Section Two: Model Essays and Writing Exercises

Writing the Persuasive Five-Paragraph Essay

There are many types of essays, but, in general, they are usually short compositions in which the writer expresses and discusses an opinion about something. In the persuasive essay the writer tries to persuade (convince) the reader either to do something or to agree with his or her opinion. For example, a writer might try to convince the reader to join a hunting organization or to stop eating meat. Or a writer might try to convince the reader that wearing fur is wrong or that medical experimentation using animals is necessary.

The Tools of Persuasion

The writer of the persuasive essay uses various tools to persuade the reader. Here are some of them:

Facts and statistics. A fact is a statement that no one, typically, would disagree with. It can be verified by information in reputable resources, such as encyclopedias, almanacs, government Web sites, or reference books about the topic.

It is important to note that facts and statistics can be misstated (written down or quoted incorrectly), misinterpreted (not understood correctly by the user), or misused (not used fairly). But, if a writer uses facts and statistics properly, they can add authority to the writer's essay.

Opinions. An opinion is what a person thinks about something. It can be contested or argued with. However, opinions of people who are experts on the topic or who have personal experience are often very convincing. Many persuasive essays are written to convince the reader that the writer's opinion is worth believing and acting on.

Testimonials. A testimonial is a statement given by a person who is thought to be an expert or who has another trait people admire, such as being a celebrity. Television commercials frequently use testimonials to convince watchers to buy the products they are advertising.

Examples and anecdotes. An example is something that is representative of a group or type (*red* is an example of the group *color*). Examples are used to help define, describe, or illustrate something to make it more understandable. Anecdotes are extended examples. They are little stories with a beginning, middle, and end. They can be used just like examples to explain something or to show something about a topic.

Appeals to reason. One way to convince readers that an opinion or action is right is to appeal to reason or logic. This often involves the idea that if some ideas are true, others must also be true. Here is an example of one type of appeal to reason:

> The Humane Society rescues many animals every year. The Humane Society needs money to keep operating. Therefore, if you love animals, you should contribute money to the Humane Society.

Appeals to emotion. Another way to persuade readers to believe or do something is to appeal to their emotions—love, fear, pity, loyalty, and anger are some of the emotions to which writers appeal. A writer who wants to persuade the reader that the use of animals in medical research is a bad thing might appeal to the reader's sense of love ("If you love animals, you will want this research to end so animals do not suffer.")

Ridicule and name-calling. Ridicule and name-calling are not good techniques to use in a persuasive essay. Instead of exploring the strengths of the topic, the writer who uses these relies on making those who oppose the main idea look foolish, evil, or stupid. In most cases, the writer who does this weakens his or her argument.

Bandwagon. The writer who uses the bandwagon technique uses the idea that "Everybody thinks this or is doing this; therefore it is valid." The bandwagon method is not a very authoritative way to convince your reader of your point.

Writing Persuasively

One way to learn to write an effective essay is to practice using a specific model. This introduction focuses on the five-paragraph essay, which has one introductory paragraph, three supporting (or explaining) paragraphs, and a concluding paragraph. The same general pattern of the five-paragraph essay (introduction, supporting paragraphs, and conclusion) can be used in essays of longer—or shorter—lengths.

The Introductory Paragraph

The introductory paragraph should do three things: capture the reader's attention, state the essay's main idea (thesis), and preview the main points the essay will make.

Capture the reader's attention. People are faced with many things to read each day—newspapers, school assignments, magazines, and more. If you want them to read your essay, you have to attract their interest. There are many ways to do this. Some include starting your essay with an interesting fact, statistic, or quotation; a shocking statement; or an interesting anecdote. But keep in mind that whatever you do, it must be tied to the key ideas of your essay.

The thesis. The thesis is the main idea of the essay. It tells the reader what you want to accomplish in the essay. In a persuasive essay, it tells the reader what you want him or her to do or to think after reading the essay. The thesis statement can be placed anywhere logical in your essay, but most often it is either the first sentence or last sentence of the introductory paragraph.

A thesis statement cannot be a fact because a fact cannot be argued. This is an example of a fact: "Many animals are abandoned and abused each year." There is nothing to debate here. This statement can easily be confirmed by checking any of a number of sources.

Instead, a thesis statement must be an opinion or something you want to convince your reader to think or do. Here are some examples:

- The best way to help abused and abandoned animals is to join your local humane society.
- Hunting helps nature regulate the wild animal population.
- You should have your pet spayed or neutered.

A thesis statement should not be too broad or you will not be able to do it justice. For example, "The government should protect animals" is very broad. This topic covers way too much territory. You will be able to do a better job if you make your topic more specific. Here's one example of a more focused thesis statement: "The government should help protect animals by providing financial support to local animal shelters."

Preview the main points. The introductory paragraph gives the reader an idea of the three main points your essay will cover. For example, using the topic sentence at the end of the previous paragraph, your three main points could be as follows: Many animals are abandoned and abused each year; There are already a lot of good animal shelters, but they don't have enough money to do all they could; The government could afford to give a very small part of its annual budget to support these shelters.

The Supporting Paragraphs

Each of the three supporting paragraphs discusses one of the three main ideas introduced in the essay's first paragraph. Each paragraph has its own topic sentence. A topic sentence is like a thesis statement, but it is the theme for the individual paragraph instead of for the whole essay.

In the supporting paragraphs, you will use one or more of the persuasive tools described in the section "The Tools of Persuasion," on page sixty-eight.

You will also need to use transitions to make the essay read smoothly. Transitions are phrases or sentences that provide a bridge between one idea and another. Sometimes they are single words or phrases like *however, of course, then, the next reason is.* . . . Sometimes they are whole sentences.

The Conclusion

The final, or concluding, paragraph sums up the essay's ideas and reinforces the thesis statement by restating it in some way. But the concluding paragraph does not simply repeat what has been said. It is the writer's last chance to persuade the reader, so it needs to show why the topic is important to the reader or what greater impact or broader implications it involves.

Factory Farms Are Inhumane

Editor's Notes The following model essay discusses factory farms and the way they treat animals. The term *factory farms* came from the animal welfare movement, which believes that huge farms treat animals more like factory machinery and products than like living creatures. Such farms raise thousands, sometimes millions, of animals for eggs, milk, and meat.

This essay is written to persuade the reader that factory farms do not treat animals well. It discusses three supporting ideas: that the animals live in tremendously crowded conditions, that the animals are bred like machines, and that the animals are treated cruelly from birth to death. Each of the three supporting paragraphs contains its own topic sentence plus supporting details and information. The essay then concludes with a summary of the main points and asks the reader to do something.

As you read, pay attention to the way the essay is organized. The sidebar notes provide additional information on the essay and its organization. In addition, consider the following questions:

1. According to the author, what is the difference between family farms and factory farms?
2. Why do you think the author includes unpleasant details about such things as chickens' beaks being cut off and animals being sent to slaughter?

Factory farms raise animals in terribly cruel conditions. In the past, most of America's food was produced on family farms. These farms were usually relatively small, and many of the families who ran them developed relationships with their animals and treated them well. But today America is fed by factory farms—gigantic acreages that raise thousands of animals. Factory farm animals live

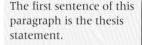

The first sentence of this paragraph is the thesis statement.

Sentences two and three provide a contrast to the writer's main topic. Writers often contrast one idea with another to emphasize qualities of one or both.

The last two sentences of paragraph one introduce the writer's three supporting ideas.

The first sentence of paragraph two is the topic sentence. Notice that the supporting information includes specific details about cage size. It also includes the effects of the crowding—disease and mental illness.

The first sentence of paragraph three provides a transition from the previous paragraph and also provides the topic sentence for this paragraph.

For supporting evidence in this paragraph, the writer describes the pig's breeding life in some detail.

in unbelievably crowded conditions. They are treated like machines, and they are treated with cruelty and brutality from the time they are born until the time they die.

Visit one of today's factory egg farms and you will be shocked by the crowding. Huge warehouses are filled with row upon long row of small wire cages stacked several tiers high. A cage just sixteen inches wide holds four hens. The hens don't even have enough space to move around, much less get any exercise. The crowding contributes to the spread of disease, which not only kills chickens but can make their meat unhealthy for humans. The crowding also leads to psychotic behavior, such as chewing on the cage wire and pecking their fellow prisoners. In many cases, their beaks have been cut off so that they cannot harm each other with their pecking. Similar conditions are found in broiler chicken and turkey farms, where huge flocks of the birds are confined in too-small, windowless sheds where the light is manipulated to make them eat more and grow big faster. They, too, have their beaks cut off and their claws trimmed so that their pecking does not cause damage to valuable bird flesh.

As horrible as the crowding are the factory farms' terrible breeding practices. A good example is on a pig farm. There, female pigs are selected at an early age to be breeders. From one year of age on through their short lives, they are made to have two or more broods of piglets each year. As soon as a pig is pregnant, she is put into a metal cage only two feet wide. It is called a gestation cage and is so small that she cannot turn around or even lie down comfortably. She is kept in this tiny cage during the four months of her pregnancy. Then when she is ready to give birth, she is moved to another cage only slightly larger. Here, she has her babies, then nurses them for two to three weeks. The piglets are taken away to a crowded piglet pen, and the mother is impregnated once again and put back into the small gestation cage. When the factory farmer decides that she is no longer healthy enough to be a good breeder, she is sent to slaughter.

As you can see, the poor pig has a very cruel life, but factory farm animals suffer many more kinds of cruelty as well. For example, dairy cows can only give milk for about ten months after they have been pregnant and borne a calf. So on a factory farm, within a day or so after a cow gives birth, her calf is taken from her so that her milk can go to humans. Toward the end of the cow's lactating period (milk-producing period), she is impregnated again so that she can continue to produce milk during most of her pregnancy. In addition, cows are given special food and drugs so that they will produce much more milk than they would normally. These foods and drugs are hard on the cow's body. In fact, a cow normally lives twenty-five years or more, but a factory-farm dairy cow lives only three or four years before she is too worn out and is sent to be slaughtered.

Clearly, the poor animals who live on factory farms live pitiful lives. Crowding, forced breeding, disease, unhealthy drugs, and early slaughter are only a few of the terrible conditions they must endure. Factory farms are inhumane, and we should all work to see that they are not allowed to exist.

Again in paragraph four, the writer uses the first sentence as both a transition and a topic sentence.

In the conclusion, the writer sums up the main points and some specific facts from the essay. The writer then issues a call to action, urging the reader to work to eliminate factory farms.

Creating an Outline from an Existing Essay

When you write an essay, it often helps to create an outline first. This helps you organize your thoughts and the information you have found in your research. Once you have a good outline, you can fill in the supporting information and, except for polishing your writing, your essay is nearly finished.

To practice, in this exercise you are going to deconstruct Essay One. By doing this, you will see how the information is organized. This will help you when you write an outline for your own essay.

As discussed in the preface to Section Two of this book, "Writing the Persuasive Five-Paragraph Essay," the first paragraph will contain the essay's thesis statement. Paragraphs two, three, and four will contain supporting information, and each paragraph will have its own topic sentence. Paragraph five will contain the essay's conclusion.

When you write essays with more (or less) than five paragraphs, you will follow a similar pattern. In most cases, the first paragraph will contain the thesis statement. (Sometimes this is not the case in a longer essay. For example, in some cases the writer might use the first paragraph for an anecdote and save the thesis statement until the second paragraph.) The following paragraphs will contain supporting evidence and information, and the final paragraph will contain the conclusion.

Below is a partial outline for Essay One. Fill in the rest of the outline.

Outline for Essay One: Factory Farms Are Inhumane

I. Thesis statement: Factory farms raise animals in terribly cruel conditions.

    A. Supporting idea 1: Factory farm animals live in horribly crowded conditions.

B. Supporting idea 2: The animals are bred like machines.

C. Supporting idea 3:

II. Supporting paragraph 1, topic sentence: . . . you will be shocked by the crowding.

   A. First evidence: Description of the chickens' crowded warehouses and tiny cages

   B. Second evidence: The effects of the crowding

     1. Spread of disease

     2. Psychotic behavior

   C. Third evidence: How factory farmers treat the results of the psychotic behavior—cut off their beaks and toes

   D. Fourth evidence: Another example—broiler chicken and turkey farms

III. Supporting paragraph 2, topic sentence:

   A. First evidence: Number of broods

   B. Second evidence: Cage sizes

   C. Third evidence:

   D. Fourth evidence:

IV. Supporting paragraph 3, topic sentence:

   A. First evidence:

   B. Second evidence:

   C. Third evidence:

V. Conclusion, topic sentence:

So-Called Factory Farms Are Necessary

Editor's Notes The following essay takes an opposite approach to that expressed in the previous essay. This essay defends the factory farm, which, in this essay, is called "the huge, modern farm." This essay was written to persuade you that such farms are the only way to produce enough food to feed the large U.S. population.

This essay incorporates several different persuasive tools. Review these tools in Section Two's preface, "Writing the Persuasive Five-Paragraph Essay." As you read, watch for the way the essay is organized and which persuasive tools are used. In addition, consider the following questions:

1. Why do you think this essay uses the phrase "modern farm"? Do you think this term is more appropriate than *factory farm*? Is either one of them totally objective—free of the user's prejudices? Explain your answers.

2. One point the essay makes is that animals must be treated differently than humans. Do you agree? Explain.

One way writers try to capture the reader's attention is by asking questions, as in the first paragraph of this essay.

Did you know that the average American eats more than 250 eggs each year? According to the American Meat Institute, we also each eat fifty pounds of pork, seventy pounds of beef, and eighty pounds of chicken each year. Where do you think all this food comes from? With more than 290 million people in the United States, there is no way that old-fashioned family farms could possibly produce it. We need today's huge, modern farms—the so-called factory farms. Animal rights activists unfairly criticize these farms that can produce the quantity of food we need and can ensure that the food we buy in the grocery store is safe.

Animal rights organizations often say that huge, modern farms treat animals cruelly. But there are laws that protect animals. If the animals were really being treated cruelly, the law would shut down these farms. Animal rights organizations say that the animals on huge, modern farms live in crowded conditions and are forced to have too many pregnancies. But the crowding and the advanced breeding practices are a necessary part of raising food for America. I believe the farmers treat their animals as well as possible or the animals would get sick and be of no use. Also, we all know that animals were put on this earth to feed and clothe humans. We have to treat animals differently than we treat humans in order for them to fulfill these purposes.

Can you find the sentences in the second paragraph that appeal to logic? Can you find the bandwagon technique? How about an opinion?

By saying that these farms produce food for America, this essay appeals to patriotism. This is a form of the appeal to emotion. Many people have feelings (emotions) of love and loyalty for their country.

In fact, if farms were not able to keep animals in compact living situations, there would not be enough space to raise enough animals to feed us. Family farms take up a huge amount of space for the amount of food they produce. And as our country has become more populated, there is less and less land available for farming. That land must be used in the most efficient way possible. So-called factory farms produced 6.33 billion eggs in December 2002 alone, according to the "Egg Industry Fact Sheet" from the U.S. Department of Agriculture (USDA). That could never be accomplished on small, family farms.

Can you find any opinions in this paragraph?

One more important thing to remember about huge, modern farms is that they use modern technology that helps keep our food safe. They inoculate animals against disease, and they have cleanliness standards they must maintain. Some farms raise animals that have been especially bred to be resistant to disease. Also, the government can inspect the farms, so that is an additional safety factor.

So you see, animal rights organizations that criticize "factory farms" have not really considered all the facts. Without huge, modern farms, Americans would not have enough food to eat. With them, we can raise the food we need and also ensure that it is safe.

Examine this concluding paragraph carefully. Does it restate the thesis? In which sentence? Does it sum up the essay's supporting ideas?

Identifying Persuasive Techniques

Essayists use many techniques to persuade you to agree with their ideas or to do something they want you to do. Some of the most common techniques are described in the preface to this section, "Writing the Persuasive Five-Paragraph Essay." These tools are facts and statistics, opinions, testimonials, examples and anecdotes, appeals to reason, appeals to emotion, ridicule and name-calling, and bandwagon. Go back to the preface and review these tools. Remember that most of these tools can be used to enhance your essay, but some of them—particularly ridiculing, name-calling, and bandwagon—can detract from the essay's effectiveness. Nevertheless, you should be able to recognize them in the essays you read.

Some writers use one persuasive tool throughout their whole essay. For example, the essay may be one extended anecdote or the writer may rely entirely on statistics. But most writers typically use a combination of persuasive tools. Essay Two does this. The sidebars point out some of the persuasive tools used in the essay.

Read Essay Two again and see if you can find every persuasive tool used. Put that information in the following table. Part of the table is filled in for you. Explanatory notes are underneath the table. (*Note:* You will not fill in every box. No paragraph contains all of the techniques.)

	Paragraph 1 Sentence #	Paragraph 2 Sentence #	Paragraph 3 Sentence #	Paragraph 4 Sentence #	Paragraph 5 Sentence #
Facts and statistics	1, 2, 4 (note 1)	1, 2, 3, 5 (note 4)			
Opinion		6, 7, 8, 9 (note 5)			
Testimonial					
Example	1, 2 (note 2)				
Anecdote					
Appeal to reason		8 (note 6)			
Appeal to emotion	7 (note 3)				
Ridicule					
Name-calling					
Bandwagon		8 (note 7)			

NOTES

1. Statistics: Sentence one—250 eggs; sentence two—50 pounds of pork, 70 pounds of beef, and 80 pounds of chicken; sentence four—more than 290 million people.

2. Sentences one and two are also examples. A number of different foods could have been written about, but the essay uses eggs, pork, and beef as examples to illustrate the essay's main point.

3. Appeal to the emotion of fear: Factory farms ensure that our food is safe; this implies that if it were not for factory farms' we would have to worry about unsafe food.

4. These statements are facts that we can verify by reading Essay One or by looking in other resources.

5. Sentence seven is clearly an opinion because it starts with "I believe . . . ." But sentences six, eight, and nine are also opinions. They are statements that some people would say are true, but animal activists—and many other people who know about farming—would not agree with them. If you did a lot of research on the ideas in these sentences, you would find that there is a lot of disagreement. This shows that they are not facts.

6. Sentence eight points out what seems logical: Factory farmers must treat their animals well or the animals will lose value. But notice that no evidence is provided to back up this logic. It may or may not be true.

7. Sentence eight is a multipurpose sentence! "We all know" tells you clearly that this is the bandwagon technique.

8. Now, look at the table you have produced. Which persuasive tools does this essay rely on most heavily? Which are not used at all?

Look back at Essay One. See if you can find any of the missing persuasive tools in that essay. As you read Essays Three and Four, watch for the persuasive tools they contain.

Animals Deserve the Same Rights That People Have

Editor's Notes The following essay has more than five paragraphs, but it follows the same general pattern that a five-paragraph essay does. You can use this kind of pattern for an essay of any length.

This essay was written to convince the reader that animals should have many of the same rights that people do—the rights of freedom, safety, and respect. In addition, consider the following questions:

1. What three ways are animals like people, according to this essay?
2. Do you think these similarities are enough to make animals deserve some of the same rights people have? Explain.

Would you eat your best friend? Or conduct experiments on her in which you cut her open while she is awake, attach electrodes to her body, or feed her drugs that you do not understand? Would you tie her to a tree and leave her alone all day? Would you film her life twenty-four hours a day, even her most intimate moments? I know I would not do these things to another person—and I would not do them to an animal either. Animals, like people, have feelings. They feel pain. And they are intelligent. They deserve to have the same rights of freedom, safety, and respect that people do.

Some people say that animals do not have real feelings. They just have instincts that allow them to react to things in their environment. I know this is not true. My Uncle Ted's golden retriever, Mitzi, was his best friend. Mitzi lived with Uncle Ted for the last ten years of his life. Mitzi was always by his side. When Uncle Ted didn't feel well, Mitzi knew it and would lay her head on his lap, offering comfort. When Uncle Ted was feeling lively, she

Notice how this essay tries to catch your attention by asking questions right at the beginning. Does it succeed—do you want to read more?

Which sentence is the thesis statement? What supporting points do you think will be expanded on in the supporting paragraphs?

What persuasive tools are used in this paragraph?

eagerly dragged him on long walks through the neighborhood. When Uncle Ted had a heart attack and had to go to the hospital, Mitzi was sad the whole time he was gone. She laid around and did not want to do anything. When he came home from the hospital, she wagged her whole body with joy, but she understood that he was still sick, so she stayed quiet and did not jump on him.

What persuasive tool does the writer use in this paragraph?

Dogs are not the only animals with feelings. Jeffrey Moussaieff Masson and Susan McCarthy wrote a book called *When Elephants Weep: The Emotional Lives of Animals*. In it, they describe situation after situation where wild and domesticated animals demonstrated genuine emotions. They tell about elephants who mourn dead members of their herd, zoo animals who suffer depression, chimpanzees who develop friendships, parrots who exhibit jealousy, and even a spider mother who shows her love for her offspring as all are dying.

What is the topic sentence of this paragraph?

Animals not only have emotions, but they feel pain. No, they cannot tell us in words when they feel pain, but many of them can communicate this in other ways: They yelp or whine, and they back up or try to get away. Also, scientists have shown that many animals have central nervous systems that are similar to those in humans. It is the central nervous system that sends messages to the brain saying that the person or animal is feeling pain. In fact, this similarity to humans is one reason scientists want to use animals in experiments: They believe they can learn about people from the ways animals react.

What does this essay use as a transition from the previous paragraph to this one?

Animals are similar to humans in another important way too: Many animals have been proven to have intelligence. They can think. They do not operate on instinct alone. Some animals can even communicate with humans. Scientists have taught apes to "talk" by using sign language or symbol boards.

Many people who say that it is permissible to use animals for food or for scientific experiments justify this by saying that humans are superior to animals. But truthfully, how superior are we? Like animals, we have emotions, we feel pain, and we are intelligent. We have more advanced skills in some areas than most animals do (e.g., we can use words, write, and make clothes and sophisticated machinery), but I do not think this is justification for killing or harming them for our own purposes. People have used the idea of superiority to justify many horrible things, including slavery and genocide. Today we are horrified to think that people ever treated each other that way. We should also be horrified that people think it is OK to treat animals that way. Animals are our fellow creatures, and we should allow them peace, freedom, and safety from those who would harm them.

Examine this final paragraph carefully. Does it sum up the ideas in the essay? Does it restate the thesis? In which sentence? Does it make a final pitch to convince you of its point of view?

Exercise Three

Writing Introductions and Conclusions

The introduction and conclusion can be the most powerful part of your essay. These two places are where you spell out what you want the reader to come away with— what you want the reader to think or do as a result of reading your essay. For some people, these parts of the essay are easy to write, but for others they present a challenge.

The key is knowing what your thesis is. If you can state that clearly, you have a big start.

Introduction. Review the information about introductions in the preface to this section of the book—"Writing the Persuasive Five-Paragraph Essay." Recall that the introduction must do three things: 1) capture the reader's attention, 2) state the thesis, and 3) preview the main supporting points. If you've written an outline, you have (2) and (3) under control. Now all you have to do is organize this material and add something to capture the reader's attention.

Go back and reread the first paragraphs of the essays in this book. Look at where the writers have placed the thesis. Look at where they've placed the supporting points. Sometimes a writer wants to start right off with the thesis statement, but sometimes the writer wants to build up to the thesis. Decide what arrangement will be most effective in your essay.

Now look at the viewpoints again. What have the writers done to try to capture the reader's attention? Asked questions? Used an anecdote? Used a shocking fact? Or something else? Think about what would be effective in your essay.

Do not worry if something does not come to mind immediately. *You do not have to complete this paragraph before writing the rest of the essay.* Go ahead and write your supporting paragraphs first if that seems easier. Then come back and finish your introductory paragraph.

Conclusion. Recall that the concluding paragraph should sum up the main points in the essay and restate the thesis. Remember: This is your last chance to persuade the reader, so if you can issue a call to action (ask the reader to do something specific) or show why your topic is important to the reader, your essay will have a stronger impact.

Go back and reread the final paragraphs of the viewpoints in this book. First look for the restatement of the thesis. Compare the way the thesis is stated in the concluding paragraph to the way it is stated in the introductory paragraph. How much are they alike? How have the writers made them different enough so that they are not just a copy of one another? Have the writers used any of the same words? A lot of the same words?

Look at the ways the writers have summed up their viewpoint's main points. In most cases, the summary in the final paragraph is probably much shorter than the statements in the first paragraph. In many cases, the writer may have devoted a whole sentence to each supporting point in the first paragraph but summed all the points up in a single sentence in the conclusion.

Take the concluding paragraph from one viewpoint in this book. Cross out the restated thesis; cross out the summing up of the viewpoint's main points. What is left? What has this writer done as a last effort to persuade the reader?

Your essay. As you write your own persuasive essay, think about the analysis you have done for this exercise. This may help you compose your own effective introduction and conclusion.

Animals Do Not Deserve Human Rights

Editor's Notes The following essay uses the persuasive technique of piling example upon example to show that animals are inferior to humans and therefore do not deserve rights similar to those humans have. This essay argues a similar point to that of Viewpoint Two earlier in this book. But notice that this essay does not copy that essay. It is organized differently, and the information is original to this essay, with one exception: Paragraph one borrows from Viewpoint Two—and tells the reader that this is borrowed information. Borrowing information from another source is acceptable as long as that source is given credit.

Note how both the introduction and the conclusion in this essay contain lists. The intent is that these extensive examples will reinforce the essay's main idea and persuade the reader to agree. In addition, consider the following question:

1. Do you agree that the lists of things animals cannot do demonstrates that animals are inferior to humans? Explain.

Notice that this essay begins with a paraphrase from Viewpoint Two earlier in this book. This essay includes a footnote that credits the original source of this information.

Animals cannot read or write, do mathematical calculations, make or play musical instruments, create or use a calendar, engage in commerce, or practice law. These are only a few of the "fifty things animals can't do"[1] that attorney and author J. Neil Schulman lists in an essay by that name. He uses this list to conclude a discussion of why animals are not equal to humans and therefore do not deserve human rights. Some animal rights advocates argue that in many ways animals *are* like

1. J. Neil Schulman, "Fifty Things Animals Can't Do," www.maninnature.com, December 7, 2000.

88

humans—they say that animals express emotion and are intelligent like humans. However, as Schulman's list indicates, there are many more ways that animals *are not* like humans. Trying to compare animals and humans is foolish. Animals are clearly inferior to humans and do not deserve human rights.

Animal rights advocates point to examples of "human-like" animal behavior by using anecdotes about loyal pets, wild animal mothers that protect their young, and chimpanzees or dolphins that scientists have taught to "speak." But if we examine these examples objectively, it becomes clear that in most cases the animals are operating by instinct or by rote. Instinct consists of the built-in mechanisms designed by nature so that species can continue to exist. It is not humanlike emotion that makes an animal mother protect her young.

Likewise, it is not humanlike intelligence that allows a chimpanzee to communicate with scientists. It is rote training. Long ago the behavioral scientist Ivan Pavlov found techniques to condition animals to behave in a way that might seem intelligent. A rat learns to find its way through a maze not because it is intelligent but because conditioning teaches it that the maze is a way to food. Likewise, a chimpanzee finds that if it pushes certain keys on a communication board, it is rewarded with praise or goodies.

Even if we were to accept that a chimpanzee can communicate in a limited way, this simply cannot be compared to human communication. A chimpanzee (or any other animal) cannot speak up and express ideas, cannot debate issues, cannot write, and cannot appreciate or use computers, cameras, and other communication media like even very young humans can.

There are a million other things that humans can do and animals cannot. All of these things add up to the simple fact that animals and humans are not equal. In fact, people have to regulate the animals that live among us. Animals cannot clean up after themselves—people have

What is the thesis statement in this paragraph? What are the three supporting ideas the essay will discuss?

Do you think the statements in paragraphs two and three are mostly facts or mostly opinions? Explain your answer.

Who is Ivan Pavlov? How does bringing him into this essay bolster the argument? What persuasive technique is this?

Notice that the concluding paragraph includes more things animals cannot do. There is no footnote this time, so the reader can assume that these were not borrowed from the Schulman essay like the items in paragraph one.

This essay's last persuasive pitch is to add more to the list of things animals cannot do, thereby reinforcing the point that animals and humans are not equal.

to do it. Most domesticated animals cannot fix themselves a meal, cure themselves when they are sick or injured, or decide what rights are. Animals cannot handle responsibility. Only people can do that. Rights and responsibility go together. Therefore, animals should not have the same rights that people do.

Exercise Four

Writing a Persuasive Five-Paragraph Essay

You have read several sample essays. Now it is time to write your own essay on animal rights. Here are six steps to help you organize your work:

1. Appendix C lists essay topics relating to animal rights. Choose one topic from the list, or make up your own. Think about what it is that you want to persuade your readers to do or think. State your idea as a thesis sentence.

2. Now you need to find information to help you make your case. You can find information in the essays in this book, at a library, on the Internet, and in newspapers, magazines, encyclopedias, books, and speeches. You can also use the resources listed in this book's appendices, bibliography, and organization list. (See Appendix B, "Finding and Using Sources of Information" for more information on this topic.) Gather your information and your notes together. Review them, and decide what information and evidence will be most helpful in persuading your reader.

3. After you have read and thought about the information you have found, decide what three main ideas will best support your thesis. (Be aware that at this point you might

have to adjust your thesis sentence. In your research you might have found information that makes you want to take a different approach. That is OK. You do not want to stick with a thesis statement that you cannot support properly.)

Write your three main supporting ideas:

1. _____

2. _____

3. _____

4. Decide how you can most effectively use the information you found. What will be the best supporting information for each of your three main supporting ideas? What tool or tools of persuasion will be most effective in crafting your essay? For example, do you have impressive facts and statistics? Will an anecdote help your reader understand the issue?

5. Now write a simple outline for your essay. (Adjust the length of this outline to fit your essay.)

   I. Thesis statement:
      A. Supporting idea 1:
      B. Supporting idea 2:
      C. Supporting idea 3:

   II. Supporting paragraph 1, topic sentence:
      A. First evidence:
      B. Second evidence:
      C. Third evidence:
      D. Fourth evidence:

   III. Supporting paragraph 2, topic sentence:
      A. First evidence:
      B. Second evidence:
      C. Third evidence:
      D. Fourth evidence:

IV. Supporting paragraph 3, topic sentence:
   A. First evidence:
   B. Second evidence:
   C. Third evidence:

V. Conclusion, topic sentence:

6. Now flesh out your essay with the information you have found and the tools of persuasion you have decided to use. Don't forget to think about a way to catch your reader's attention in the first paragraph, use transitions to make your essay move smoothly from one idea to the next, and make your final paragraph a strong last pitch for your idea.

Section Three: Supporting Research Material

Facts About Animal Rights

Editor's Note: These facts can be used in reports or papers to reinforce or add credibility when making important points or claims.

Animals and Biomedical Research

- In 1986 the U.S. Congress's Office of Technology Assessment estimated that 17 to 23 million animals are used in the United States for research each year. Ninety-five percent of these are rats and mice bred for research.
- In 2000 the U.S. Department of Agriculture's *Animal Care Report* stated that 69,516 dogs and 25,560 cats were used in research.
- According to a *Wall Street Journal* article in 2002, wildlife biologists report that more than 1 million animals are killed by automobiles each day—more than 365 million per year. This is far more than the number used in biomedical research.

Source: Foundation for Biomedical Research (www.fbresearch.org).

Three Common Animal Tests Used in Medical Research

- *Draize test.* The test substance is placed in the eyes of conscious albino rabbits, usually without anesthesia. The resulting eye damage is observed. This test is used to predict if the substance will cause skin or other irritation in humans.
- *Skin irritancy test.* The test substance is applied to shaved areas of an animal's skin to determine sensitivity.
- *Acute toxity test.* This test, also called the Lethal Dose 50 test, determines how much of a substance is needed to kill 50 percent of a group of test animals.

Source: Animal Protection Institute (www.api4animals.com).

Three Alternatives to Animal Tests in Medical Research

- *Use of lower organisms.* Researchers use invertebrates (such as worms), plants, microorganisms (such as bacteria and yeast), chicken eggs, and frog embryos for some research, but these only work for early information about a process, not for more complex studies.
- *Imaging techniques.* Very advanced brain- and body-imaging techniques, such as PET scans, are used to provide information about the effect of chemicals on the brains of living rats and mice.
- *Computer studies.* Researchers use computer and mathematical modeling to predict interactions between chemicals (such as medicines) when used on people and animals. But these studies are limited by the previously known information that is fed into the computer and cannot predict such things as a medicine's side effects.

Source: Medical Research Council (www.mrc.ac.uk).

Examples of Medical Advances Obtained Through Animal Experimentation

When	What	Animal Used
1726	First measurement of blood pressure	Horse
1790	Smallpox vaccine	Cow
1880	Anthrax vaccine	Sheep
1888	Rabies vaccine	Dog, Rabbit
1923	Insulin discovered	Dog, Fish
1933	Tetanus vaccine	Horse
1945	Penicillin tested	Mouse
1954	Polio vaccine	Mouse, Monkey
1956	Open-heart surgery and cardiac pacemakers	Dog
1982	Treatment for leprosy	Armadillo
1989	Organ transplantation advances	Dog, Sheep, Cow, Pig
1995	Gene transfer for cystic fibrosis	Mouse, Nonhuman Primate
2001	Promising AIDS-prevention drug developed	Monkey

Source: Foundation for Biomedical Research (www.fbresearch.org).

Nine Common Food, Medical, and Other Ingredients That Come from Animals

- *Adrenaline.* A hormone taken from hog, cattle, and sheep adrenal glands. Used in medicine.
- *Angora.* Soft fibers taken from angora goat or rabbit fur. Used in sweaters and other clothing.
- *Benzoic acid.* Found in all vertebrate animals and in berries. Used as a preservative in toiletries such as deodorant, mouthwash, and aftershave.
- *Bone meal.* Made from crushed animal bones. Used in fertilizer.
- *Casein.* A milk protein. Used in cosmetics, soy cheese, and nondairy coffee creamers.
- *Gelatin.* A protein made from animal skin, hooves, bones, and tendons. Used in gelatin and pudding, candies, ice cream, vitamins, and photography.
- *Insulin.* From hog pancreas. Used to treat diabetes.
- *Lanolin.* A fat from sheep wool and oil glands. Used in skin care products, cosmetics, and medicines.
- *Musk oil.* A dried secretion from the genitals of musk deer, beaver, otter, and certain other animals. Used in perfumes and food flavorings.

Source: People for the Ethical Treatment of Animals (www.peta.org).

Finding and Using Sources of Information

When you write a persuasive essay, it is usually necessary to find information to support your point of view. You can use sources such as books, magazine articles, and online articles.

Using Books and Articles

You can find books and articles in a library by using the library's cataloging system. If you are not sure how to use these resources, ask a librarian to instruct you. You can also use a computer to find many articles written specifically for the Internet.

You are likely to find a lot more information than you can possibly use in your essay, so your first task is to narrow it down to what is likely to be most usable. Look at book and article titles. Look at book chapter titles, and take a look at the book index to see if the book contains information on the specific topic you want to write about. (For example, if you want to write about the fur industry and you find a book about animal rights, check the chapter titles and index to be sure it contains information about the fur industry before you bother to check out the book.)

For a five-paragraph essay, you don't need a great deal of supporting information, so quickly try to narrow down your materials to a few good books and magazines or Internet articles. You don't need dozens. You might even find that one or two good books or articles contain all the information you need.

You probably don't have time to read an entire book, so find the chapters or sections that relate to your topic, and skim these. When you find useful information, copy it onto a notecard or into a notebook. You should look for supporting facts, statistics, quotations, and examples.

Evaluate the Source

When you select your supporting information, it is important that you evaluate its source. This is especially important with information you find on the Internet. Because nearly anyone can post information, there is as much bad information as good information. Before using Internet information—or any information—try to determine if the source seems reliable. Is the author or Internet site sponsored by a legitimate organization? Does the author have any special knowledge or training related to the topic you are researching? Does the article give any indication of where its information comes from?

Using Your Supporting Information

When you use supporting information from a book, an article, or another source, there are three important things to remember:

1. *Make it clear whether you are using a direct quotation or a paraphrase.* If you copy information directly from your source, you are quoting it. You must put quotation marks around the information and tell where the information comes from. If you put the information in your own words, you are paraphrasing it. Sometimes you must tell where you got this information, and add a footnote documenting its source.

Here is an example of a quotation:

"The number of dogs that go missing each year under suspicious circumstances has been conservatively estimated by shelters and pounds, animal-protection organizations, and veterinarians to be in the hundreds of thousands. Puppy-mill breeders and the organizers of dog fights buy their share, but the animals also end up subjects in the biomedical-research industry, which pays top dollar."[1]

1. Judith Reitman, "From the Leash to the Laboratory," *Atlantic Monthly*, July 2000, p. 17.

Here is a brief paraphrase of the same passage:

In an article in the *Atlantic Monthly*, writer Judith Reitman states that animal welfare organizations report that hundreds of thousands of dogs disappear each year, only to be purchased by puppy mills, dog-fight organizers, and biomedical researchers.

2. *Use the information fairly.* Be careful to use supporting information in the way the author intended it. There is a joke that movie ads containing critics' comments like "First-Class!" "Best ever!" and other glowing phrases take them from longer reviews that said something like "This movie is first-class trash" or "This movie is this director's best ever—and that isn't saying much!" This is called taking information out of context (using it in a way the original writer did not intend). This is using supporting evidence unfairly.

3. *Give credit where credit is due.* You must give credit when you use someone else's information, but not every piece of supporting information needs a credit.

- If the supporting information is general knowledge—that is, it can be found in many sources—you do not have to cite (give credit to) your source.
- If you directly quote a source, you must give credit.
- If you paraphrase information from a specific source, you must give credit. If you do not give credit where you should, you are plagiarizing—or stealing—someone else's work.

Giving Credit

There are a number of ways to give credit. Your teacher will probably want you to do it one of three ways:

- Informal: As in the second example in number 1 above, tell where you got the information right in your essay.
- Informal list: At the end of the essay, place an unnumbered list of the sources you used. This list often has

the heading "References." This tells the reader where, in general, you got your information, but it doesn't tell specifically where you got any single fact.

- Formal: Use an endnote or footnote, like the first example in number 1 above. (An endnote is generally placed at the end of an article or essay, and a footnote is placed at the bottom of the page on which the information you are crediting occurs.)

Your teacher will tell you how information should be credited in your essay. Generally, the very least information that you will list for a source is the author's name and the name of the article or other publication.

Be sure you know exactly what information your teacher requires before you start looking for supporting information so that you can include this information as you take notes.

Sample Essay Topics

General
Animals Should Have the Same Right to Freedom as Humans
Animal Life Is Less Valuable than Human Life
Pets Should Be Spayed and Neutered
People Who Abuse Animals Should Be Sent to Jail
We Should Spend Our Resources on People, Not Animals
Animal Rights Activists Are Terrorists
Animal Rights Activists Protect Animals

Animals in Research
Medical Research Needs Animals
Medical Researchers Can Get the Same Results from Nonanimal Methods
It Is Better to Test Products on Animals than on People
Animal Research Should Be More Carefully Regulated
It Is OK to Use Animals like Worms, Fruit Flies, and Rats in Research
Even Animals like Worms, Fruit Flies, and Rats Should Be Protected from Inhumane Experimentation
Dogs, Cats, and Rabbits Should Not Be Used in Experiments
Researchers Treat Animals Humanely
Boycott Companies That Use Animals to Test Their Products
Dissecting Animals Is an Important Part of Biology Class

The Food Industry
People Who Love Animals Should Stop Eating Meat
Humans Have the Right to Use Animals for Food
"Factory Farms" Should Be Abolished
We Need Large Farms to Feed the Nation

The Clothing Industry
The Fur Industry Treats Animals Humanely
Trapping Animals for Fur Should Be Banned
People Should Not Wear Fur or Leather

Organizations to Contact

American Society for the Prevention of Cruelty to Animals
424 E. Ninety-second St., New York, NY 10128-6804
(212) 876-7700 • fax: (212) 348-2088
Web site: www.aspca.org

This organization promotes the humane treatment of animals and works to pass and enforce anticruelty laws.

Americans for Medical Progress
908 King St., Suite 201, Alexandria, VA 22314-3067
(703) 836-9595 • fax: (703) 836-9594
Web site: www.ampef.org.

This organization's mission is to protect society's investment in medical research. It promotes public understanding of and support for the appropriate role of animals in biomedical research.

Association of the British Pharmaceutical Industry (ABPI)
12 Whitehall, London SW1A 2DY, UK
44 (0)20-7930-3477 • fax: 44 (0) 20-7747-3477
Web site: www.abpi.org.uk

The ABPI represents some one hundred British pharmaceutical companies. Its Animals in Medicines Research Information Centre provides information and education about the use of animals in medical research.

Farm Sanctuary
PO Box 150, Watkins Glen, NY 14891
(607) 583-2225 • fax: (607) 583-2041
Web site: www.farmsanctuary.org

This organization rescues abused or abandoned farm animals and campaigns against factory farms and cruelty on farms and in stockyards and slaughterhouses.

Fund for Animals

200 W. Fifty-seventh St., New York, NY 10019

(212) 246-2096 • fax: (212) 246-2633

Web site: www.fundforanimals.org

Founded in 1967, this organization works for the welfare of wild and domestic animals throughout the world.

Fund for the Replacement of Animals in Medical Experiments

Russell & Burch House, 96–98 N. Sherwood St., Nottingham NG1 4EE, UK

44 (0)115 9584740 • fax: 44 (0)115 9503570

Web site: www.frame.org.uk

This organization works for the reduction of animal use in medical research. Its ultimate aim is to stop the use of animals in research, but in the meantime, it works to both minimize animal use and animal suffering.

Fur Commission USA

PMB 506, 826 Orange Ave., Coronado, CA 92118-2698

(619) 575-0139 • fax: (619) 575-5578

Web site: www.furcommission.com

The Fur Commission represents mink farmers and works to ensure responsible animal care and to educate the public about fur and the fur industry.

Humane Society of the United States

2100 L St. NW, Washington, DC 20037

(202) 452-1100 • fax: (202) 778-6132

Web site: www.hsus.org

This organization works to develop respect, understanding, and compassion for all creatures. It promotes responsible pet ownership and the elimination of cruelty to animals.

Incurably Ill for Animal Research
PO Box 27454, Lansing, MI 48909
(517) 887-1141 • fax: (517) 887-1710
Web site: www.iifar.org

This organization works to ensure the continued use of animal testing to find cures for diseases such as cancer and AIDS.

Medical Research Council (MRC)
20 Park Crescent, London W1N 4AL, UK
44 (0)20-7636-5422 • fax: 44 (0)20-7436-6179
Web site: www.mrc.ac.uk

The MRC supports animal use in well-designed studies that are likely to provide new information about human health. It promotes ethical values in animal use, including their housing and care and the elimination of animal use when other effective experimental methods are possible.

People for the Ethical Treatment of Animals (PETA)
501 Front St., Norfolk, VA 23510
(757) 622-7382 • fax: (757) 622-0457
Web site: www.peta.org

PETA works to establish and protect the rights of all animals and focuses primarily on research laboratories, the fur trade, the entertainment industry, and factory farms.

Performing Animals Welfare Society (PAWS)
PO Box 849, Galt, CA 95632
(209) 745-2606 • fax: (209) 745-1809
Web site: www.pawsweb.org

Founded in 1985, PAWS provides sanctuary to abandoned and abused performing animals from circuses, zoos, rodeos, the exotic animal trade, and other entertainment venues.

Bibliography

Books

Daniel Cohen, *Animal Rights: A Handbook for Young Adults.* Brookfield, CT: Millbrook, 1993.

Helen Cothran, ed., *Animal Experimentation: Opposing Viewpoints.* San Diego: Greenhaven, 2002.

Patricia Curtis, *Animal Rights.* New York: Four Winds, 1980.

Laura Fraser, *The Animal Rights Handbook: Everyday Ways to Save Animal Lives.* New York: Berkley, 1993.

Trudy J. Hanmer, *The Hunting Debate: Aiming at the Issues.* Berkeley Heights, NJ: Enslow, 1999.

John J. Loeper, *Crusade for Kindness: Henry Bergh and the ASPCA.* New York: Atheneum, 1991.

Finn Lynge, *Arctic Wars: Animal Rights, Endangered Animals.* Trans. Marianne Stenback. Lebanon, NH: Dartmouth College, University Press of New England, 1992.

Kathleen Marquardt, with Herbert M. Levine and Mark La Rochelle, *Animal Scam: The Beastly Abuse of Human Rights.* Washington, DC: Regnery, 1993.

Ingrid Newkirk, *You Can Save the Animals.* Rocklin, CA: Prima, 1999.

Tamara L. Roleff, ed., *The Rights of Animals.* San Diego: Greenhaven, 1999.

Peter Singer, *Animal Liberation.* Hopewell, NJ: Ecco, 2002.

Kim W. Stallwood, ed., *Speaking Out for Animals.* New York: Lantern, 2001.

Periodicals

Bowhunter, "Alaskans Fight for Bear Hunting," December 2004.

Heidi Brown, "Beware of People," *Forbes*, July 26, 2004.

Economist, "Playing Terrorists: Animal-Rights Extremism," April 17, 2004.

Lancet, "Animal Research Is a Source of Human Compassion, Not Shame," September 4, 2004.

Barbara Righton, "All the Sad Horses," *Maclean's*, February 10, 2003.

Internet Sources

AMRIC, "Non-Animal Methods." www.abpi.org.uk/amric/basics.asp.

Animal Welfare Research Center, "Questions and Answers About the Animal Welfare Act and Its Regulations for Biomedical Research Institutions," U.S. Department of Agriculture Library. www.nal.usda.gov.

Association of the British Pharmaceutical Industry, "Animal Research and Human Medicine: A Resource for Schools." www.abpi.org.uk.

Jane Chastain, "Why This Bunny Will Wear Fur Again," December 4, 2003. www.furcommission.com.

Fur Harvesters Auction Inc., "Myths & Facts of the Fur Industry." www.furharvesters.com.

Sandra Gotlieb, "It's Safe to Wear Fur Once More: Animal-Rights Folk Have Lost the Ability to Intimidate," *National Post* (Canada), February 21, 2004. www.furcommission.com.

Las Vegas Review-Journal, "Mauling Brings Out the Nuts," October 12, 2003. www.reviewjournal.com.

Medical Research Council, "Mice and Medicine," July 2000. www.mrc.ac.uk.

Jim Motavalli, "Down on the Filthy Farm," *E/The Environmental Magazine*. www.emagazine.com.

Pete, "Animal Rights vs. Animal Welfare," San Francisco Indymedia, January 19, 2005. http://sf.indymedia.org.

Philadelphia Inquirer, "Stop Activist Criminals," July 17, 2002. www.amprogress.org.

Teresa Platt, "Saving Society from Animal 'Snuff' Films," Fur Commission, February 6, 2004. www.furcommission.com.

Seattle Post-Intelligencer, "Animals & Research: A Five-Part Series," April 16–21, 2000. http://seattlepi.nwsource.com.

J. Neil Schulman, "Fifty Things Animals Can't Do," December 7, 2002. www.maninnature.com.

———, "The Illogic of Animal Rights," 1995. www.maninnature.com.

Index

Picture Credits

Cover Images: Photos.com;
  © Carl & Ann
  Purcell/CORBIS (inset)
AFP/Getty Images, 31
© AP Photo/Georgia State
  University via Des
  Moines Register, 19
AP/Wide World Photos, 8,
  11, 12, 16, 25, 32, 35,
  48, 51, 56, 60

Getty Images, 22, 38, 45
Victor Habbick, 36, 42,
  55
© Ed Kashi/CORBIS, 41
National Geographic/Getty
  Images, 9
Time Life Pictures/Getty
  Images, 28
© Michael S.
  Yamashita/CORBIS, 64

About the Editor

Terry O'Neill is a writer and editor who has contributed to many Opposing Viewpoints books. She is a former teacher of English and the current editor of an engineering trade magazine.